StarDreaming

Letters from a Mystic to a Science Fiction Author

CollectiveInk

First published by Sixth Books, 2026
Sixth Books is an imprint of Collective Ink Ltd.,
Unit 11, Shepperton House, 89 Shepperton Road, London, N1 3DF
office@collectiveinkbooks.com
www.collectiveinkbooks.com
www.6th-books.com

For distributor details and how to order please visit the 'Ordering' section on our website.

ISBN: 978 1 917704 62 5
978 1 917704 63 2 (ebook)
Library of Congress Control Number: 2025912240

www.maureenbroberts.com

A CIP catalogue record for this book is available from the British Library.

Design: Lapiz Digital Services

UK: Printed and bound by CPI Group (UK) Ltd, Croydon, CR0 4YY
Printed in North America by CPI GPS partners

The manufacturer's authorised representative in the EU for product safety is: eucomply OÜ - Pärnu mnt 139b-14, 11317 Tallinn, Estonia, hello@ eucompliancepartner.com, www.eucompliancepartner.com

StarDreaming

Letters from a Mystic to a Science Fiction Author

Maureen B. Roberts

6TH
BOOKS

London, UK
Washington, DC, USA

This book features a recollection of events and inner experiences that centre around my relationship with Damien Broderick and several impactful Dreams I experienced between 1994–7. To the best of my knowledge, I have not included any material that could be construed as damaging to reputation, defamatory, invasive of personal privacy, libellous, or in any other way harmful to any person.

In gratitude to all the deep loves of my life, and with fond memories of Damien Broderick, whom the world lost several months after I completed this book.

Contents

Acknowledgements

I extend my appreciation to all the authors, scholars, colleagues and friends mentioned in this book, without whom these 'letters' would not exist. My heartfelt thanks go to beloved author and Jungian scholar Alice O. Howell, for her friendship over many years, and for so kindly adopting me as her spiritual daughter — and her own biological daughter's 'twin'. I am grateful to Dr Haydn Williams for mentoring me with ongoing support, wise advice, friendship and encouragement throughout my scholarly and mythopoeic meanderings. During my undergraduate days, Haydn's lyrical Welsh accent lured me to his inspiring university lectures on classical English literature.

Above all, to my Dad I offer boundless gratitude and love. In my childhood it is he who instilled into me my deep, abiding love of writing, music, Nature, art, imagination and photography. I am thankful, too, to my Mum, from whom I inherited my passion for singing, dancing, long walks and reading. To C. G. Jung, whose writings fatefully came into my life during an acute spiritual crisis — when I was almost lost to the Abyss — I am eternally grateful. Jung appeared to me in several important dreams throughout the years that followed when he helped me to remain true to the unique law of my own being.

Finally, I am indebted to the following, from whose publications I have included brief quotations: Penguin Books Ltd for *The Magician's Nephew*, by C. S. Lewis; William Morrow & Co. for *Transformation: The Breakthrough*, by Whitley Strieber; Inner City Books for *Alchemy: An Introduction to the Symbolism and the Psychology*, by Marie-Louise von Franz; Warner Books for *Queen of Angels*, by Greg Bear; Tom Doherty Associates LLC for *Red Orc's Rage*, by Philip José Farmer; Orbit Books for *Against a Dark Background*, by Iain Banks; Millennium Orion Publishing Group for *Permutation City*, by Greg Egan; Donald

I. Fine, Inc. for *Neverness,* by David Zindell; Jonathan Cape for *The Crystal World,* by J. G. Ballard; Tor Books for *The Stars in Shroud,* by Gregory Benford; and Princeton University Press for *The Collected Works of C. G. Jung.*

Introduction

I'd forgotten that I still had these letters until I discovered them while dumping obsolete files from my laptop. Because I'd also forgotten almost the entirety of their content, re-reading them was like discovering material written by someone else. I no longer recalled not only the details of certain events from that crucial phase of my life, but also most of the science fiction texts I mention. As a result, poring over the letters decades after writing them has been mesmerising, entertaining, refreshing, enlightening and heartwarming.

I have no qualms about confessing that I like the rediscovered writer of these letters immensely; she's someone I'd be glad to call a friend, confidante and scholarly colleague. One cannot, after all, genuinely love others without loving oneself, warts and all. Sadly, at the time of writing the letters I didn't have the kind of undemanding love for myself that has since become a liberating and healthy norm. In retrospect I don't regret that former flaw, given that it was my willingness to be wounded which kept me in the relationship which spawned the letters, even when that vulnerability became almost too painful to bear.

Around that time, as a longtime member of the Mythopoeic Literature Society of Australia [MLSA], I had newly acquired a passion for the science fiction literary genre. I had also recently been awarded my PhD degree; my supervisor, an avid science fiction devotee, had introduced me to several novels that resonated with the Jungian slant of my thesis. In no time I was hooked and took to devouring one science fiction novel after another. It didn't take me long to recognise that science fiction at its best was contemporary mythology which – by bridging science and imagination – spoke to our collective dreams, defects, aspirations, and search for identity, transcendence and meaning. Science fiction interwove many of my core passions:

the Cosmos, the heroic 'quest' motif, philosophy (as the 'love of wisdom'), mysticism, archetypal themes, myth-making, the battle between good and evil, spirituality and the evolution of consciousness. Thrilled to find out that the MLSA was set to host an international science fiction conference at the University of Melbourne, I hesitantly yet keenly put up my hand to be one of the speakers.

The paper I presented at the conference briefly explored science fiction as contemporary mythology that reflects the evolution of a collective consciousness inextricably bound to technology. I referred to numerous works of science fiction, including well-known Australian author Damien Broderick's novel *The Dreaming Dragons.* Widely regarded as Australia's 'dean of science fiction', Damien had amassed an impressive body of work that included his cyberpunk novel *The Judas Mandala,* which coined the term 'virtual reality' in 1982. His award-winning *The Dreaming Dragons* featured in David Pringle's *Science Fiction: The 100 Best Novels* [1949–84] and was chosen as the year's best by Kingsley Amis.

Unbeknown to me, Damien was present in the conference audience. During a break in the proceedings, he approached me and we chatted for a short time. As I recall, I was not at all attracted to him physically, or emotionally; romantically he just wasn't my type. He initially came across as a self-assured, softly spoken, shrewd, guarded and supremely intelligent man, full of brilliant insights but lacking the kind of emotional warmth and intensity that resonated with my own heart. Damien's outer coolness, I later learned, was in part a defensive *persona,* a self-protective, surface 'mask' beneath which lurked a deeply poetic soul.

We all adopt masks of one kind or another in social situations where we do not feel safe, or comfortable with exposing and expressing our true selves. The persona is thus an integral facet of a healthy psyche, but to identify with it is to sell our soul in order to fit in, be feared or admired, or seen as socially respectable. It can also be a way for sensitive, wounded souls to armour themselves against the possibility of being further hurt by others, a theme which surfaces in my later letters. The persona then becomes a twin-edged sword, since we cannot give and receive genuine love without being vulnerable to the pain it inevitably inflicts.

After the conference I returned to my hotel room and went to bed early, since I needed to get up at dawn the next day to catch my return flight to Adelaide. That night I had an overwhelmingly powerful, precognitive Dream that was in essence a highly condensed, symbolic dramatisation of my entire relationship with Damien — including an indication of how it would end. I have discussed the Dream in some of the letters, but I never shared with Damien its ending. His final move was to quickly wheel himself away from me, downhill in a wheelchair propelled by his burnt hands and stunted arms. Enough said.

When I awoke I was stunned and disoriented. But before proceeding further, I'll mention that I'm capitalising 'Dream' because during the years 1994–97 I experienced a deluge of intense activity within my psyche, which gave rise to a series of inordinately powerful Dreams that were unusually vivid, and emotionally either devastating or extremely disorienting. The Dream of Damien had been so real, clear and disruptive that I found it next to impossible to focus on the mundane task of getting ready to leave the hotel. I was so dazed that I almost forgot to book a taxi to the airport. In all honesty, if it hadn't been for the Dream I wouldn't have given my rather cerebral chat with Damien a second thought. Yet now I'd been hit with an overview of a deeper relationship that hadn't yet begun.

Once back in Adelaide, I found myself routinely wandering about in an unfocused, limbo-like state, caught between something that had in one way already happened but not yet manifested outwardly. It was like living in two realities, neither of them more real to me than the other. Eventually I contacted Damien and we decided to start exchanging letters. A couple of months later, one of my PhD supervisors invited me to mind his house while he and his wife went on an overseas trip. It was while staying here that the phone rang one evening. I knew it was Damien, but as I got up to answer the phone my legs gave way beneath me and I collapsed to the carpet, the first and only time that such a 'fall' has happened. I often wonder if it was a kind of synchronicity — a physical mirroring of the destabilising impact that this relationship was to have on me.

Damien told me on the phone that he wanted to fly over for a visit, which I happily agreed to. When he finally arrived on my doorstep with a bottle of champagne, I opened the door and announced, 'Here he is, the man of my dreams'. I of course meant it literally rather than figuratively — and certainly not idealistically, given that I was well aware of how the Dream had ended.

Particularly when it came to romantic relationships with men, one of my weaknesses at that time was to go out of my way to please, praise and support them, or keep the peace at all costs, all too often at the expense of my own emotional health. While I never compromised my personal integrity, I often ignored the emotional pain, worse still the masochism that often came with not being loved for who I was. I'm nonetheless eternally grateful to Damien for playing devil's advocate by embodying a great deal of my then repressed, unconscious shadow. By the same token, in retrospect I can see that I was too accommodating toward some of his more disagreeable proclivities. And perhaps he would have said exactly the same about me. What I know is that through embracing the discomforting challenge he represented, I became in time a more well-rounded individual.

It's always been my *modus operandi* to move on once a transformational phase has ended, by completely severing ties to whatever, or whoever is no longer essential to my personal

Tao. There's an element of the inner *daemonic* at work here, too; that relentless hunger to 'follow one's bliss'—the beckoning call of one's heart—wherever it may lead. Accordingly, since emotionally I've now moved on from my relationship with Damien, I can appreciate these letters from a detached standpoint that weighs their merit in terms of their potential interest to readers. Lovers of science fiction, Jungian scholars, analysts and therapists, holistic philosophers, scientists, and practitioners of mysticism, shamanism, and spiritual healing should find much to interest, amuse, inspire, challenge, enlighten, or intrigue them.

Because the original files are decades old however, a sizeable chunk of text has been irretrievably scrambled, or otherwise corrupted beyond repair. As well, I've omitted material that I consider to be too private to share, in terms of it being either too personally explicit, or potentially embarrassing to either of us. In addition, to preserve the anonymity of certain folk Damien and/ or I knew, I have abbreviated their names to invented initials. Hopefully the text I have retained suffices to convey a sense of the emotional complexity and tension which our temperamental quirks, background experiences, and different takes on life generated.

It could be argued that these letters have validity only if Damien's input is included. I beg to differ. Firstly, this is primarily an autobiographical rather than dialectical offering; secondly, the letters in many places respond or allude to Damien's implied, or inferred input; thirdly, the insights and reflections I offer draw upon psychospiritual, developmental and relational truths and experiences that many readers will hopefully relate to. Finally, both emotionally and psychologically the tone of Damien's letters differed markedly from my own. Sometimes cynical, he was also a more extraverted, disciplined, grounded and rational person that me. My focus is more on the inner life and transformation of the psyche, irrational intuition, dreams, myth, mysticism, synchronicities, spiritual experiences and insights, and Jung-oriented insights into relationships.

Based on my personal experience and understanding, the mystic is 'one with all' not by choice, but as a result of a movement of grace that opens the heart and inward eye of vision to the direct intuition of all reality as the symphony and dance of universal Tao. For the mystic, there is no division between self and God, since mystically the experience of 'God' is synonymous with the intuitively sensed centre of our own being, which I call the 'divine self'.

Mysticism is a unifying consciousness that transcends spacetime and is immersed in the unitary Ground of Being. From this vantage point, there are essentially no discrete beings but rather endlessly creative versions of the One Energy, or Cosmic Soul. For the mystic, this One Soul is the living sea in which they and all beings swim. Through observing this play of forms and soul, the mystic remains aware of the ceaseless flow of energy into and out of its tangible and imaginal expressions. Through contemplation and meditation, s/he constantly communes and is one with the circumferential whole of Nature and Cosmos.

I shared little about my own mystical experiences with Damien, mainly because of his conscious aversion to anything that (to him) smacked of naively optimistic New Ageism. Because the first few letters were written before he flew to Adelaide to spend time with me, their tone leans toward cordiality and friendliness. After he returned to Melbourne, our amusing anecdotes, witty banter, scholarly discussions, swapping of news, and philosophical musings gradually gave way to much deeper, emotionally volatile exchanges. To cope with the demands of this descent into tension, my own self-protective persona became very much the antithesis of the Medusa-like, seething, secretive core of my true self: light-hearted, optimistic, intellectual and detached. I suspected that the unleashed, passionate intensity of the real me would have scared the hell out of Damien. Heck, at times it scared me.

Emotionally, intellectually, spiritually and physically, I experienced our relationship as a kind of Jungian analysis. And analysis, far from being a calm, rational evaluation, can be a challenging, close interaction between two people who, because of their equal force of character and personality differences, push one another so far out of their comfort zones that a mutual shattering, or 'dis-integration' unfolds. Analysis, in other words, breaks the whole into constituent ingredients and dissolves one's illusion of having a stable, fully understood, predictable, or safely inscribed psyche.

Thus while I strove to keep an emotionally even keel that I felt might keep the relationship afloat, I could not stave off what in time became a jumble of combative, affectionate, conciliatory, defensive, and ultimately dismissive and angry responses to my letters. Hence 'e-motion', which includes tension and conflict, is the raw material for the alchemy of mutual transformation. But it is love which warms the alchemical 'Work'. Take that away and Mercurius, the mysterious 'Unseen Third' in an analytical relationship, no longer has the energy to catalyse further meaningful change. In the end, whatever love Damien may have had for me turned cold, or was forcibly suppressed.

I'm largely in the dark as to how he experienced all of this, and whether it left a lasting impact on him in terms of a needed transformation of his own psyche. I've never doubted that because our unorthodox, at times bizarre relationship was fated to happen — and because I followed my heart in allowing it to unfold in its own way — only good came of it. I hope, then, that you enjoy these letters as much as I revelled in writing them.

The final 'AfterWords' section of this book speaks for itself and revolves around several other 1994–7 Dreams that fatefully disrupted my life. With regard to Ayrton Senna, that impact still resonates deeply throughout my heart and soul.

Maureen B. Roberts, PhD

1994 Letters

1 September 1994

Dear Damien

Thanks for your letter, which I received along with an upbeat reply from La Trobe UP concerning your *Theory and Its Discontents*. They said they'd let me know the publication date when the 'formal decision' to publish it has been made. I'm pleased to hear, too, that your radio play is punningly receiving some final fine-tuning. As I see it, though, the obvious trouble with 'Schrödinger's Dog' as a title is that, well, it sounds German, whereas 'The Wind at the Edge of the World' has a distinctly Australian feel to it. Besides, how many potential listeners will be drawn in through picking up the allusion to Schrödinger's Cat? The original title, on the other hand, would probably sound poetically alluring to a potential audience. Still, I haven't read the play, so of course am not really qualified to judge which title does justice to its content.

Have you come across the following two books which someone recently recommended to me: *Music of the Mind* and *The Death of Forever*, both by Darryl Reanney and apparently on quantum physics? My problem is that because I work only part-time, I can't afford to buy many books but must instead confine myself to begging and borrowing — I haven't resorted to stealing yet — from friends and libraries. Still, the pros of part-time work include having plenty of time to read lots of science fiction [sf] books. I've been at it pretty solidly for over a year now, so I'm still very much at the toddler stage, which translates into digesting as much good stuff as I can, without overloading my brain.

I've also just been absorbing a book on the marvellous Ainslie Roberts (sadly, no relation of mine). The mythic basis of one painting — *Mangowa and the Round Lakes* (1964), which features godlike cosmic hands reaching forth from the galaxy — struck me as having robust potential for a science fictionalisation of Dreamtime myth, perhaps in a vein similar to your *Dreaming Dragons*. The myth in a nutshell: 'Pursuing the lovely Pirili, whom he loved, Mangowa the hunter followed her into the sky, tearing down handfuls of stars from the Milky Way as missiles to drive her back. Pirili eluded him in the end, but the stars fell on the earth and formed the round lagoons that fringe the shores of the coastal lakes of South Australia'.

Significantly, I recently had a dream about taking a bus trip to one of these lagoons. As we drove, I could see beneath the bus the sacred animals that 'followed' the Songlines of the Dreaming through the Land. When I arrived at the shore of the lagoon, very large, black hands — dotted all across the surface — reached up out of the water in a kind of greeting.

Another potentially sf-inspiring work by Ainslie is *Birthplace of the Moons*, for my money the most serenely and astonishingly beautiful painting I've ever come across.

Incidentally, I don't actually have a degree in astronomy; it's just one of my main passions and was a subject I took as part of my science degree, for which I majored in botany and zoology. I've always been intrigued by the mystery, complexity and diversity of Nature, which is why sf's extrapolations of it into new planetary and/or stellar contexts fascinates. As an outcome of my degree, I went on to do field research in marine and river ecology and helped to produce a major study of River Torrens flora and fauna, as well as studies of various seaweed and desert plant communities.

I like your term 'black holists', but — aside from deplorable New Age rip-offs — what about the issue of holism as a re-emerging episteme? I wish I could talk with you more about this. What I mean is, why oh why does there keep resurfacing throughout the history of Western thought the intuition of a subterranean stream of innate archetypal ideas? It seems to me that we're witnessing in our age the supersession of the poles of mysticism and technocracy by something which unites them both, perhaps some sort of equivalent to Kant's transcendental substratum, Tao, the Plotinian One, the collective unconscious, call it what you will. As one instance, the multifarious uses of quartz crystal perhaps symbolise a bridging of the gap between what in ultimate reality could be merely a semantic distinction between science and magic. Isn't this loosely implied, admittedly with comic irony, in your *Sea's Furthest End*? Holism, in other words, subverts the dualism based on several falsehoods, namely the myths of objectivity, of egocentricity (as the self isolated from the universe), and the supremacy of reason (over intuition).

Of course you know a lot more than I do about the scientific side of all this, but in terms of a general trend isn't it true that to delineate the qualities of the new scientific paradigm, rather than resort to logic we must instead evoke paradoxes in that the theoretical emphasis is no longer on analysis, but rather on interaction, complementarity, synchronicity, paradox and relatedness, reflecting the supposition that matter, energy and consciousness have a common ground which is unknown? In relation to this we have Leibniz's proposal that an underlying metaphysical unity generates the phenomenal realm; Bergson's belief that the underlying primary reality can be comprehended only through intuition; Whitehead's claim that the mind-matter dualism is false, while reality is holistic; not to mention Bohr's principle of complementarity and the Jung-Pauli hypothesis of synchronicity, which posits a psyche-matter continuum that subverts the materialist view of the universe.

Still, it all remains weird, wonderful and mysterious, and of course open to endless speculation. I must say, though, that at the Mythopoeic Conference I was rather annoyed by N's glib dismissal of the likes of Paul Davies and *The Tao of*

Physics, an attitude that to me smacks of academic snobbery which assumes that because an idea is popular or (heaven forbid) understandable by anyone with modest intellect, it must therefore be completely wrong.

More recent reading:

Christopher Priest, *A Dream of Wessex* (nightmarishly Phildickian)
Sladek, *The Reproductive System* (hilarious!)
The Müller-Fokker Effect
Anna Kavan, *Ice*
Robert L. Forward, *Dragon's Egg* (fun — I love anything about pulsars — my favourite phase of stellar evolution)
Cherryh, *Angel with the Sword*
Zelazny, *Lord of Light* (finally I've read it!)
Connie Willis, *Doomsday Book* (engrossing, moving and painstakingly researched)
Ian Watson, *The Martian Inca*
Kate Wilhelm, *Margaret and I*
Herbert, *The God Makers* (better than the curious *Whipping Star*)
Gibson, *Mona Lisa Overdrive*
Niven, *A World Out of Time* (not one of his best, and too sexist for my liking)
Ballard, *The Day of Forever* (excellent Twilight Zonish short stories)

Zelazny's is a wonderful novel, lovingly detailed and carefully crafted, although he misses the opportunity to exploit — as you do so brilliantly in *Sea's Furthest End* — the ontological facets of Hindu philosophy. Incidentally, I read Crowley's *Aegypt* last year and enjoyed its philosophical labyrinths immensely; it's an example of a work that rewards close reading, and I agree with you that many readers nowadays want to be spoon-fed and so fail to appreciate the challenge and reward of reading literature of substance.

I'm still not sure what to make of Gibson's books, though. The novels abound with surface glitter, but come across (to me, at least) as rather thin on plot and psychological substance. As well, although I admire his consistency of vision and style, his antiseptic overstatement of visual imagery sometimes blurs, or detracts from the plot.

It strikes me, actually, that cyberpunk can be seen as a subversion and inversion of myth; that it is, therefore, an anti-myth of sorts. For if in the cyberpunk world 'myth' is the technocratic lie which lures us falsely to equate image with an implied underlying reality, in genuine myth the inverse is true in that the literally unreal (myth) does convey an underlying symbolic, or metaphoric truth. As well, if myth is integrative, or holistic in function, anti-myth expresses the (perhaps) necessary disintegration of cultural dominants which results in a fragmentation of consciousness and culture. Still, maybe I've missed Gibson's point somewhere along the line.

I saw the letter you mentioned from *Science Fiction* #35, and felt that T's criticism of *Striped Holes* was vague and purely subjective, besides which what on earth could he have meant by 'self-indulgent'? Looking through some of your typed pages I note, by the way, that your 'Faustus Hexagram' has evolved (via a Pentagram) from a four-novelled tetrahedron, with no loss of clarity as to your schematic intent. Why not consider using an inverted bipyramid to accommodate the six novel vertices? Then, when you've completed seven novels, the addition of a singularity-type centre might fit the bill and would, to boot, reflect the Chinese philosophy of the added direction of 'Centre'. Hence on to a cube for no. 8, centred again for the ninth, and so on. Of course, the good thing about all your playful juggling of theory is that you adapt the theory to the facts — the facts being your works — instead of squeezing (like critical theorists tend to do) the text into the coffin of a desiccated, inflexible perspective.

Intermission: here's a draft of a poem:

In Memory of Philip K. Dick

Through rust-hinged doors of ruined lands
I gazed upon an open book scratched
with desperate diagrams for where to go
Looking suffices till the word steels forth
to stress the times again
Skyward drift fond ashes of remembering
we were once a chosen people till
destruction danced in streaming fire
along our weary veins
Elastic stretch of infinite horizon
fallen towers torn and stacked like soldiers slain
debris and damnation intertwine

Settle the tilting stem upright
propped against a mote-infested wedge of light
we wait for thunder
race against the turning tide
dust still makes us cry
Who lied and why?
What twists of fate have coiled so tight
to sever once certain connections?
Save the fragile outcrop of a sunless place
take whatever comes upon the morning wind
and fleeing the country of the lost
where the dispossessed run free
voyage to our island homes along a heaving shore.

A couple of interesting events: I was recently invited to give some talks on sf to 10 year olds at a primary school. It went over extremely well and I was pleasantly surprised at how responsive, informed and bright these kids were, more so, sadly, than most adults I know. In fact they were so keen that they persuaded the teacher to invite me back for more. When I turned up in the school library the first words I heard came from one kid calling out to another, 'Where's the science fiction books?' — so I knew I was in my element. Also, next week composer Malcolm Fox will be talking and showing videos at the Mythopoeic Literature Society on his operatic adaptation of Ted Hughes' *The Iron Man*. Our local branch of the MLS was an offshoot of the 1990 Oz-wide conference called 'Imaginings', which some colleagues and I hosted at Adelaide Uni, and at which I gave a (ludicrous) paper on the connection between Romanticism and quantum physics.

And now, for the fun of it — and triggered by your final injunction to 'Watch the skies!' — I'll tell you a bit more about that powerful Dream I mentioned having on the last night of the Melbourne Mythopoeic Conference. The mandalas I mentioned occurred in the following context: in the first part of the Dream you and I were sitting at a table outdoors — possibly on a university campus — and two other people, whom I didn't recognise, were nearby. It was night time and in the sky two alien craft, which looked like stars, were rapidly orbiting each other in a complex interweaving. Then I (and I assume you also) suddenly lost awareness of outer reality and we were telepathically imprinted with a rapid series of mandala images, which I (at least) somehow knew originated from the alien objects (all very Phildickian, I'm sure you'll agree). The defining lines of the mandalas seemed to be constructed of some sort of thin, luminous wire, variously coloured and apparently technological in origin. When this telepathic 'imprinting' suddenly ended, I asked you how much time had elapsed and you looked at your watch and said, 'Ten minutes'. (And this, as I recall, was roughly the length of time I spoke with you after I'd given my Conference talk.)

In terms of ultra-real clarity, fateful impact and overwhelming emotion, the only comparable Dream I've ever had occurred four months ago, when I precognitively experienced the fatal crash of Formula One World Champion, Ayrton Senna. I was privileged to meet him briefly at last November's Australian F1 Grand Prix, where he kindly autographed a photo for me. Knowing that he was deeply spiritual, I then said to him, 'May God be with you on Sunday' (the main race day), unaware that this would be his last ever Grand Prix win. Some five months later in the Dream, my consciousness was present in his racing car during his final lap before the crash, and then finally (and horrendously) as it crashed into a wall. I woke up in shock, grief and trauma, certain that it was Ayrton, and knowing that he'd been killed. About an hour later the terrible crash (at the San Marino Grand Prix) was seen live on TV.

Needless to say, I was utterly devastated, as were billions of folk worldwide. The whole thing was and still is intensely gut-wrenching, given that Ayrton was such a sensitive, generous, highly evolved and beautiful soul. It feels, though, like he's still around, not in any sort of ghostly way, but more as if he's a Bodhisattva who's chosen to return to the world out of compassion.

Incidentally, I'm intrigued by your description of what's involved in your writing journeys. However, if you balk at me (justly) praising your writing, I'll no doubt make you even more uncomfortable by praising you instead, namely by saying that I see in you a good heart. If you don't care to acknowledge this truth then the blind spot is, I suggest, perhaps evidence of such goodness, by which I don't imply any kind of moral superiority, but rather the rare capacity to empathise and articulate the tragicomical heights and depths of the human condition.

Well, I always seem to wax whimsical and pseudo-philosophical toward the end of letters, so I'll go with the flow and do so again by confessing a truth that would be abhorrent to many academics, namely that I love having a completely empty mind, a state I've cultivated into becoming pretty much the norm. This *via negativa* often leaves me with the sense of having nothing to say, that is, the sense that what is self-evidently truthful need not, or cannot be confined to words. 'The Tao that can be explained is not the true Tao.' Here Nature is more articulate than mind, since it mirrors the mind in its seasonality and creative tension of extremes; hence through the cross-pollination born of counterbalance one (ideally) learns to think with the heart and feel with the brain. But to summarise, Nature is 'unfathomable ... because it is the "letting be", the creative outpouring, of the Infinite'. (Sound familiar?) Anyway, here's my last autobiographic word on the matter, namely a bit of light late night reading, perhaps to be savoured during the ads while *Star Trek* or *Quantum Leap* is on TV — from the 'Fruit for Thought' Department — and dedicated to John Keats, who coined the term 'Negative Capability', which is the ability to reside in mystery and uncertainty without needing to rationally explain it.

THE DEATHMELON

The Deathmelon rolled its blind rind-spots to Heaven
'I see it all clearly', it said,
and giving a squish of self-comforting glee
rolled back to its dark soil bed.
What joys, what horrors, what wonders it knew
in its Godlike stance mute, yet invincible,
what terrors passed by it, so quiet and round
in its spherical trance, unconvincible.
For it needed no knowledge, its knowledge no need
expressed, since its life simply was.

It said next to nothing to itself
(overheard by the lettuce, Cos.)
It was a Deathmelon and wanted to be
no other creature or fruit,
for what did it need but the sky and the land
and the light and the water to boot?
It was its own point and circumference too,
its nothingness all that it had,
for its Negative Capability seemed
to most others quite foolish or mad.
But it knew what all other fruit-veggie things know
and it saw what potato eyes see,
how the vine deep in anchoring soil must lie
that Deathmelons may roam about free.
The Deathmelon, peaceful and undisturbed,
snuggles down in the soil to sleep
till the Sea beckons once again
and it sets its heart on the briny deep.
For therein is the greatest treasure of all —
the huge Pearl like a Deathmelon shaped,
and the rickety old wooden garden fence
is transformed to the Pearly Gate
as the Deathmelon dreams
while the pattering rain falls down soft
like a meteor shower
and the Deathmelon wakes 'neath a thin slice of Moon
in a nothing and everything hour.
It stretches its rind, contented, looks up
where beyond the leaf silhouettes, free,
the planets like ripening pearls sail on
as the Deathmelon dreams of the Sea.
Now the rain patter stops
like the crackle of fire retired to an emberous glow,
and the Deathmelon, winsome and joyfully sad,

seeks no other existence to know.
For it knows that it knows not,
it sees its own Point,
its invisible focus of sight,
and it wraps the soil darkness about itself
and stares up at the stars of the night.
For it is a Deathmelon, it ebbs and it flows
rolled about by the tides of Desire,
and the end of its longing is, Sun and Moon-like
to rise like a round Phoenix from Fire.

I just watched the pilot episode of a new series, *SeaQuest DSV*. The sets and special effects were well done, but the plot and characterisation were rather predictable —the obligatory whizz-kid, the German-accented baddie versus American hero — that sort of thing, plus rather too padded out with dialogue, and a bit like an underwater version of *Deep Space Nine*. Still, it may get better as it as it goes along.

In closing, your Flaubert-bending definition of sf is the best I've yet come across, namely that sf is 'a cracked test tube we whistle tunes across, moved to pity and laughter by the stars, and by all the poor souls beneath them'. (I enjoyed typing that!)

Blessings

P.S. 'Our life is no dream, but perhaps it ought to become one, and one day will.' (Novalis)

18 September 1994

Dear Damien

Thanks for your letter and enclosures which I received in the midst of pottering about to the stirring strains of Pachelbel's 'Canon in D'. Talk about multiplying synchronicities — now it's your closing reference to hippie-mimicking. I'd just been removing painted flowers from my face, after recovering from the ordeal of masquerading as a hippie to attend my sister-in-law's '60s style' birthday bash. 'Hey, man' – I'm quoting from your new radio play here. Not being a party person (I prefer quiet candlelight dinners), I found the whole affair rather tiresome, although the 60s music was nostalgically pleasant. Who was it said that if you remember the 60s you weren't there? Well, whoever said it was wrong, since I, for one, was certainly there and I well recall being completely whacked out for much of the time. Now, of course, it all seems like something that happened to someone else in another universe. Still, I suppose for some of us Blake's proverb applies: 'The road of excess leads to the palace of wisdom'. (Interesting that Blake features in Farmer's *Red Orc's Rage* and Ballard's *The Unlimited Dream Company*.)

Some Indian friends of mine (i.e. from India), both Uni lecturers, have just been raving enthusiastically to me on the phone about your *Sea's Furthest End.* I loaned them a copy a few weeks ago. Thanks for letting me know about *Time Zones*; it was good to hear your voice again. I set up a tape to record the play, which I found absorbing from the start. Given that you included so many warm and amusingly human touches, you worked in Heisenberg and the theoretical side unobtrusively, and deftly avoided overstating the necessary abstractions. I felt that the acting veered toward melodrama at times, though, especially the lead male role. What's happening with 'Schrödinger's Dog', by the way?

I picked up the phrase 'lies breathed through silver' from an essay by Tolkien in which he quotes C. S. Lewis as having quoted it to him, but Lewis typically doesn't cite his source, since he was fond of assuming that everyone would know it anyway. Like you I'm an infinitely lapsed Catholic, but in my old Christian days I used to read Lewis all the time and confess to still adoring his space trilogy. I was also recently intrigued by the discovery that embedded in his *The Magician's Nephew* is a double metaphor for wormhole travel. Basically it involves a mediating, timeless 'no-place' called 'The Wood Between the Worlds' which operates as a spacetime gateway. By jumping down and through a pool there, the kids in the story end up in another world in another universe. One of the characters draws an analogy between the wood and a tunnel that runs under the roof for the entire length of the connected homes that make up the building he lives in. As he says about the tunnel: 'It isn't a room in any of the houses. In a way, it isn't really part of any of the houses. But once you're in the tunnel you can go along it and come out into any of the houses in the row. Mightn't this wood be the same? — a place that isn't in any of the worlds, but once you've found that place you can get into them all?'

Anyway, I'm wondering if Lewis's intuitive insights might come in handy if I get more opportunities to speak to primary school kids. The other relevant notion is that for Lewis 'The Wood Between the Worlds' is obviously an allegory of the Christian Cross as what he regarded as the central Still Point of history — the singularity again!

Getting back to holism, I believe our age is rediscovering a certain ambiguous principle of reality, namely an intermediary state of existence transcending both matter and mind, objective and subjective. Picking up on Mailer's point (which you quote) that science involves 'the poetic impulse to treat metaphor as equal to equation', Lewis, for one, lamented that the medieval 'onion rings' spherical model of the universe had become not merely a 'Discarded Image', but simultaneously disproven as scientific fact. Yet, as his dear friend Owen Barfield notes (in his *Saving the Appearances*), the real revolution in astronomy was its instigation of 'a new theory of theory', which involved the separation of fact from a holism that saw no need to distinguish fact from symbolic appearance. In some sense it seems, then, that in recent years our ideas concerning the nature of the universe have come — in a punningly literal way — full circle, with the theory of 'curved space' which gives rise to a model that is neither objectively visible as such, nor merely symbolic. The spherical 'appearance', in other words, as a model combines, or rather transcends, both the literal and the figurative. This is where the God *archetype* comes into play, through its manifestation as 'centre and circumference'. If the God archetype is the collective sphere, the centre is where we each are individually, since experientially the God archetype coincides with Jung's archetype of the 'self' as the true core of our being.

Through the branching off of scientific empiricism in the late Renaissance, fact and symbol emerged as opposing modes of truth. In *Paradise Lost*, for instance, Milton scorns the fruitless efforts of those who contrive to 'save appearances' by attempting to prove the literal sphericity of the cosmos. Yet to save the appearance by regarding it as mere fact was to undermine its authority as a model which had never laid claim to factual verification.

Whereas metaphor works as analogy, symbol implies identity in that the activation of an archetype generates a particular mode of perception and existence, a *subjective certainty and universality* as what I'd call 'symbolic reality'. Hence from Blake's perspective, for instance, the earth is concave — viewed from within — rather than convex. Inside his visionary landscapes we are within hollow spaces, such that the sky is an 'immortal Tent'. See, it's all crystal clear, and you thought our 'differing mindsets' could 'run into terminal antinomies' and whatnot.

I've been slowly re-savouring *The Judas Mandala* with orgasmic relish. How exquisitely your imagination is tuned to the delicately poised nuances of life, from the soiled to the sublime. Your work is fulfilling to read because it prompts a response on the emotional, aesthetic, atmospheric, and conceptual planes. (I won't settle for less than all four.) As well, it comes across as being unabashedly subsumed by the

Trickster archetype — God's favourite masquerade — because it juggles and synthesises all the antinomies of life, such as the poles of 'abstraction and flesh-scented warmth'. This is all very wonderful, and maybe you need to be reminded of it as such; as Greg Benford says in his Afterword to *The Stars in Shroud*: 'Writers play the God game with their books. Weary, they will see a plastic epiphany where other, fresher faces sense a true revelation. That's the business'.

Your description of Sriyanie's first experience of teleportation sounds like what I've recounted to you — my childhood waking nightmares of my bedroom collapsing inward to a terrifying point of infinite density — equivalent to the archetypal self as the Gnostic point/singularity; namely, when she 'undergoes catastrophic implosion, the universe recedes, she suffers ultimate, singular density'. Significantly as well, in my first (dreadful) attempt at a novel (1983) — which was called *The Cross Connection* and concerned two parallel, interfacing realities, one causal, the other synchronistic and symbolic — my main character was named 'Siraihne', which sounds a bit like your Sriyanie.

I had a good laugh at some of your short story pseudonyms, especially Roger Delany, Alan Harlison, Horace West, and Iago Yarrick. Last week I had a go at the first of Antony Swithin's 'Rockall' Chronicles (remember him at the Mythopoeic Conference?). It's a fairly straightforward quest narrative, solidly researched in terms of medieval authenticity, though rather too staid for my more adventurous taste.

I've read almost all the Hugo winners now, though I still haven't managed to get hold of the Lois McMaster Bujold books. Here, as requested, are a few 'salient details' for you: I did a BSc at Adelaide Uni, before which I worked as a graphic artist and photographer. I still do quite a bit of (mainly) ink line drawing and last year had some of it published in a New York anthology, *Air Fish*. In 1986, in partnership with Oz's top shutterbug William Yang, I covered the media photography for the Adelaide Festival of Arts.

I'm sorry to hear that my squishy poem 'worried' you. I assure you it was only meant to make you laugh. Okay, I'd have settled for a smile, even a wryly amused grin, being as it was merely a bit of light nonsense, which was the 'whole point'. I appreciate the constructive feedback, though. Perhaps you're lucky I didn't send you, as I originally intended to, an even more ludicrous, long ballad, 'The Rind of the Ancient Deathmelon', a parody of Coleridge. And I concede that 'steels forth/to stress' is being too clever by half. Speaking of PKD, *Total Recall* was on again last week. Given the relatively quiet nature of Phil's short story, it's a shame they dragged in all the violent padding, which only served to detract from the original cognitive theme. Have you noticed, as well, that in the opening credits they had the gall to spell Philip as 'Phillip', which they also did at the end of *Blade Runner*?

On the work front, in the past year it's been a challenge for me to attempt to liven up the inherently dull subject I teach at the University of SA. Since a fair proportion of the students are doing Chemical Engineering degrees, the imaginations of many of them are confined to wondering who will win the next Grand Final. But there are always the odd few who appreciate the need for the *educare* of bringing forth what is latent within. A major essay assignment I gave them last week included a question on the use of metaphor and non-verbal communication in the (5th Season) *Trek: TNG* episode, 'Darmok', which I screened during a lecture. One student, who'd sent a *TNG* episode he'd written to Paramount, gave a ten minute talk on how the Enterprise warp-drive, phasers, and tri-corders work. I assure you I gave him no encouragement!

On the subject of our favourite show (as closet Trekkers), I'm glad that you, too, enjoyed the closing scene of 'A Fistful of Datas'. I similarly experienced a leap of delight at that wonderful shot and, since I'd taped the episode, replayed it several times.

Another neat ending occurred last week in the episode about Holmes' mortal enemy, Moriarty, manipulating the holodeck; at the end came a brief scene of two planets colliding to form a new star. *Deep Space Nine* has just started screening here. The pilot episode, involving a stable wormhole, had a reasonably sophisticated plot, but subsequent episodes don't live up to the initial promise.

I'm on-side with your response to Paul Davies' *The Mind of God*, since I've always felt that being stuck in the Western trappings of dualism and causality, he pushes an awkward blend of pseudo-Christian theism and physics. The two simply don't mix. As I see it, though, Hawking's self-explanatory universe doesn't conflict with an acausal, synchronistic view of the cosmos, since with the latter the notion of the transcendent 'otherness' of 'God' is replaced by the immanence of 'Eros' as the Grand Unifier. In this connection, I guess I've always been concerned with getting to the heart of things — and people — and I know that underneath all the arguable surface detail Something Indefinable And Unifying is going on; furthermore, no-one would be able to convince me otherwise.

By the way, a couple of years ago I shared a fascinating lunch with Paul Davies and a friend. Citing quantum principles of observation, Paul launched into a detailed explanation of why the table we were sitting at probably wasn't there if we weren't looking at it. I was equally convinced that it was, for the simplistic yet irrefutable reason that I could feel it with my eyes shut. (Believe it or not, this stumped him.)

I've mentioned the cosmic paintings of Ainslie Roberts. Ironically, the editorial to a recent issue of *Astronomy* magazine mentions 'the dreaming myths of the Aboriginals, which are small, often contradictory stories dealing with small slices of reality....' And speaking of useful ideas for sf, further on I came across a photo of spiral galaxy M51, which has a striking dark 'X' that marks the exact position of its central black hole. Perhaps one could posit that a technologically superior culture formed the X as some sort of 'marking the spot' ploy for the benefit of extra-galactic civilisations. The same issue discusses the Mars 'Observer' mission, which is still mapping the planet, but why, I wonder, don't they suggest an investigation of the Pyramids and Face? What sane person, after all, can resist the lure of the carrot before the donkey of desire for mysterious horizons that beckon to the questing heart?

You're justly angered by the pervasive sentimentality and woolly thinking of quantum 'quackpots', and judging from your review and reply to Goodwin, Reanney's book falls into that category. However — and I hope I don't incur your wrath by saying this (though I'm prepared to risk it) — I sense that underneath your incisive criticism of the works concerned you have other, far more personal fish to fry, perhaps related to your past. And if saying that doesn't anger you then the following, which I also 'saw' in that Dream, probably will: beneath your sometimes tough and angry exterior lies a sensitive, wounded and emotionally vulnerable man (all very appealing, dare I suggest). I do know that if your heart is, as I have glimpsed it to be, a 'glowing jewel lying on the breast of the desert', mine is a dark pearl lying at the depths of the ocean. One encounters strange and wondrous things here, felt as the transitory brushing of a fin, then melting into silence. And even more so than music, silence comes closest to expressing the inexpressible. In which case I'd best say no more, except to wish you, as I always do, the very best that life cares to toss up onto your shore.

7 October 1994

Dear Damien

I thought that all my birthdays were arriving all at once when I found your package propped on top of my letter-box. Then, before I could recover from the thrill of this discovery, I opened the letter-box itself and was further elated to find another letter from you. They must both have come at the same time owing to the public holiday here on Monday.

Thank you for taking the time to write such enjoyable letters, and for sending me the typescript of *Reading By Starlight.* The other day I'd come across (in a bookshop) mention of its imminent release and was wondering whether it was a work of criticism, or fiction. I feel immensely privileged to receive a copy before it's reached the stage of being hot off the press! Looking through the intriguing Contents listings, though, makes me realise what an ignoramus I am. I suppose this comes from being a self-emptying mystic, who is unable, indeed unwilling to retain too many facts or ideas in my head — except the idea that there are too few facts — and the fact that there are, in the world at large, too many ideas.

My brain has indeed been getting a big workout (and loving it, as Maxwell Smart would say), in savouring and sifting through your ideas, though. I've just finished *The Architecture of Babel,* a spirited and eloquent delineation of the transience and limitations of different modes of knowledge and discourse, which I thoroughly enjoyed. In view of my own response to your fiction, which I recently described as combining 'a ruthless compassion and a sensitive brutality', I appreciate your comment that 'works (or texts) are neither exquisite refinements nor brutal assaults, but are rather on some level, within the dialogue of writer and audience, both' (p. 36). I can't imagine why you should feel at all 'flattered' by anything I say about your writing, by the way. My comments always seem to me superfluous in the face of the sheer brilliance of your mind and imagination. Yet below and beyond this, I always retain when reading your work what I have mentioned before: the sense of my heart resonating with yours on some secret, subterranean, pangalactic level of communion.

I enjoyed hearing about your fun and games with stoves, though I sympathised with your horror at being roused from a quiet morning slumber, since I firmly contend that there's absolutely nothing worse than having to get up early in the winter. 10 am-ish is a sensible and proper time to stagger forth and face the day, especially for those of us who habitually burn the midnight oil. Still, it's just as well that your 'offending cooker' was found out, otherwise you might have ended up with terminal asphyxiation. Come to think of it, maybe it was leaking gas that triggered your Hypnopompic Reverie(?).

What wonderful news that you've been promised 30 grand for 1995. I should think so, too. The last thing a writer of your calibre wants to be forced to think about is money, right? I hope this generous handout frees you to be able to get on with whatever gems are brewing in your creative depths. (That wasn't a mixed metaphor, rather an allusion to the drinkable jewels of the subterranean land of Bism in C. S. Lewis's *The Silver Chair*.)

I'm glad you've been enjoying my recorded songs, and that your favourites are mine, too. I appreciate your kind comments about my yearning for the stars; even stifling Protestant dogma didn't manage to quell that. Thanks, therefore, for being gracious enough to overlook the Christian overtones in my lyrics. I never consciously tried to emulate anyone at the time, though I've always been a great admirer of Kate Bush, Carly Simon and Joni Mitchell. And C. S. Lewis, ever the literary chameleon, lifted the title 'Surprised By Joy' from Wordsworth. You mentioned Samuel Barber's Violin Concerto. I'm not familiar with it, but on the strength of your recommendation perhaps we could get hold of a copy when I see you again and listen to it together. After all, what would life be without music? Answer: dull, soulless and inarticulate. My favourite composers include Britten, Gershwin, Chopin, Mahler, Rachmaninov, and Monteverdi.

Your quote from *Mistress of Mistresses* — my favourite fantasy novel of all time — is intriguing; I hadn't noticed it before. On a personal level I can relate to it, since as I've described to you, I used to live this 'inward condensation' as a primal phase of individuation. My later dream of being the central figure of a spiral galaxy was an elaboration of this as the next developmental phase, if one views the galaxy as a mandala with a 'centre and circumference' God-structure. This relates to my point (excuse the pun) about the self as an archetype coinciding symbolically with the core galactic black hole singularity. Jung's stuff on UFOs, with which you mention having suddenly connected, is pertinent here, that is, UFOs as distorted mandalas that presage psychic wholeness as the emergent dominant of our collective consciousness, an idea which, as you'd know, Fritz Leiber alludes to in *The Wanderer*.

Your mentioning Rory Barnes is a bit synchronistic, too, since along with your letters I received a note from the local library informing me that they'd finally tracked down a copy of your and Rory's *Valencies*, so I now have this volume to look forward to as well. You mentioned good old P W, a bluff, shrewd and likeable guy, and a self-styled philosopher, though in a rather reductionist and Skinnerish psychological vein. I know him vaguely, since I sat in on his and T's sf course last year, where I was often to be seen and heard heckling from the sidelines when either of them said something I vehemently disagreed with, which was often enough. A couple of years back I sent P a politely rude note complaining about the total lack of women writers in the course, added to which I jokingly enclosed a photo of Dr Who (the Jon Pertwee version) glaring scathingly at an alien monster. I don't think P has ever forgiven me for this.

What good news that you're thinking of heading over this way. You can't imagine how much I look forward to seeing you again, given that the last time I saw you was in a hugely impactful Dream. Candlelit dinners — what fun; and I just received (as an early birthday present from my folks) a new candelabra, one of those tall, black ones with five holders. My place is a bit cramped, unfortunately, but if you can spare a day or so from your writing schedule and have the inclination, I know of a very special, small and quiet retreat in the hills, which I'd be more than happy to share with you.

I sympathise with your frustration over delays in the publication of your *Theory and Its Discontents*. How dreary, time-wasting and exasperating editing phases (and people undertaking them) can be. I've suffered the same fate with *The Diamond Path*, my book on Keats, which has finally been accepted for publication by UP of America in Maryland. I'm pleased, of course, that they've agreed to publish it, but I get the feeling that all the dithering about with reformatting, editing, contract querying, getting copyright permissions and whatnot that I still have to do, might end up taking longer than it did to write the thing in the first place.

Harvard UP are being specially tiresome and finicky with regard to me quoting their text of Keats' poems. It's kinda ironic, I feel, that poetry which sprang with such fluid spontaneity from the passioned depths of someone's soul should end up being bogged down in the red tape of copyright laws. Still, it'll probably be worth the effort to be able to sit back and watch the waves this book might cause in Romantic circles, given that my reading of Keats is diametrically opposed to the entire existing critical consensus. Of course, once I get this book out of the way I'll be free to get on with other things. Which brings me to your flattering suggestion that I attempt a study of your fiction.

I must say that I'm honoured, firstly that you should think me capable of such a worthy enterprise, but more that you should trust me enough to want me to subject your works to my (probably bizarre) critique of them. I hope it need not be said, though, that the enthusiasm for such a challenge is already there, and in fact has been hovering about me ever since the Melbourne Conference. To tell the truth, though, I have doubts about my ability to do the job, but I know I'd at least give it my best shot. Of course, as perhaps you'll agree, there would be a definite advantage in working with the author on this. I'm led to this suggestion once more by that Dream I had of us, various aspects of which I've unfolded to you as it has seemed timely to do so. Not surprisingly, your suggested title *Dreaming The Stars* connects meaningfully with the Dream, since its opening 'scene' was of the two orbiting stellar objects in the night sky. It has since 'dawned' on me — and other elements of the Dream support this interpretation — that these two stars, which were rapidly interweaving in a complex dance, represented you and me, and that the accompanying kaleidoscopic succession of mandala images mirrored this meaning. (The whole Dream unravelled like some sort of symbolic time compression sequence.)

Since it feels right to divulge what follows, I can tell you that a later section of the Dream ran as follows: you were writing something about flowers (hopefully not a novel about hippies!). Someone handed me a large bunch of flowers, at which point I broke into tears and said to you: 'You are doing what I've always wanted to do'. There was no sadness at all in this, rather a sense of joy over your superior writing ability, and over the realisation that I was involved in a supportive way in your writing, since in the Dream it was my task to count the stems and tell you how many there were. This sounds a bit like Psyche's mythic task of sorting, but the stems also reminded me of *I Ching* divination stalks. The overriding impression was that we were both 'servants of the gift' — the gift being your awesome talent as a writer — and that we were achieving more together than we could as lone individuals. As I've mentioned, my Dream of Ayrton Senna's fatal crash and my later Dream about you are the two most powerful and unsettling dreams I've ever had. Still, I suppose stranger things have happened, though I have yet to hear of them. In fact, I wouldn't mind betting that ol' PKD was behind both shattering dream events.

When I arrived back in Adelaide after the conference, I felt a deep conviction that somehow I was to become involved in your writing. I'm well aware that I'm playing the Holy Fool by revealing what I so far have about this Dream, but in spite of the feeble protestations of my mind, I'm constrained to do so by a deeper inner authority which can neither be named, nor denied. Of course if this Dream, whatever its origin, is 'true', then you, too, will recognise it as such. That said, I confess that since experiencing the Dream (or did the Dream experience me?), my heart has been constantly with you — I don't know how else to describe the reality — during which time I've felt a profound peace, even, dare I suggest a sense of belonging. Does all this sound stupid, sordid, strange, or surprising, or perhaps all four, to you?

On the subject of dreams, last weekend I attended a stimulating Blake Conference which T organised at Adelaide Uni. It amazes me, though, that all the Blake scholars I've met are sceptical about paranormal phenomena such as synchronistic dreams, visions and revelations, given that Blake himself was a renowned visionary. As a child he saw angelic beings sitting in trees, for instance. Anyway, after the conference some of us went to dinner at T's place. During this pleasant evening I dropped a clanger when I casually remarked that I'd met C. G. Jung — and myself as a Doppelgänger — in a dream. Nothing unusual in this, I always thought, but everyone scoffed at it, kindly yet patronisingly. I then added insult to injury by mentioning that I'd also met Tolkien and C. S. Lewis in dreams. I met Lewis after one of his Oxford lectures, when I shyly approached him with the manuscript of some science fantasy material I'd written, then tentatively asked if he'd consider looking over it, which he graciously agreed to do. (I still haven't had any feedback!) I suppose I could have really got them going if I'd told them about my Dream of you and me and the cosmic mandalas.

Small news items: Last week I gave a 20 minute interview on sf for the ABC, which was enjoyable. I gave our Oz writers a big push, natch, specially you (as 'our best sf writer'.) I've just finished Sean McMullen's *Voices In The Light*, Terry Dowling's *Blue Tyson* (I admire his peculiar brand of mythogenesis and his creative use of Jungian themes), and Delany's marvellous *Nova*. I was also impressed by another recent read, a (1991) sane and balanced book by F. David Peat on chaos, synchronicity, Hilbert space and whatnot, called *The Philosopher's Stone*. Using holistic principles of quantum mechanics, he even proposes a solution to the Schrödinger's Cat dilemma. I haven't read much on the UFO abductions which you've been researching, but it's a fascinating topic to be sure. I've had around twenty dreams in which I was being looked for, or pursued by alien craft. They haven't caught me yet!

Recently I came across a lacklustre, sedate limerick in a (now obsolete) book on black holes by John Taylor (1973):

There was a young lady called Bright
Who could travel much faster than light
She went out one day
In an Einsteinish way
And returned on the previous night.

This is no match for your cleverer, bawdy limerick on black holes in *Transmitters*, a book whose raw honesty and stark energy hit many a nerve in my memory and imagination.

A few weeks ago I managed to get away for a couple of days to the YHA at Inman Valley, from where I did some tramping along the coast and the Heysen Trail, before returning to light campfires at night. It's food for the soul to re-centre and remind oneself of the simplicities that matter, namely, to savour all that life (as Tao) has to offer, to regret nothing, to embrace and serve truth in all relatedness, to strive for the excellence that all these mortal pangs demand and deserve. There's nothing quite like gazing out to unreachable cloud islands and up to knotted ribbons of high-flying gulls, thence to lone hawks slowly stitching up the sky with invisible threads of air. And why, I wonder, do such marvels evoke such deep feelings of nostalgia?

Take care.

Fondest wishes

17 October 1994

Hi there Day (to my Dark)

It was good to hear from you, as always. I warn you at the outset that this letter will take a weirdly mythic slant. Our intertwining in a Dream as dancing stellar objects seems to be spot on, since it's now becoming clearer that we're each integral to one another's personal mythology. Intriguing yet baffling stuff here, even by Jungian standards, and you appear to be ready to accept that your own myths are perhaps more autobiographical than you've acknowledged them to be until now.

It seems to be growing clearer that if I'm part of your 'quest for the feminine', you are fulfilling a complementary role in my own quest for the masculine. To begin with, though, I don't subscribe to Toni Wolff's reductive categorisation of women into four types, since in my view this fourfold schema is another convenient subdivision of the feminine *anima* archetype. The most common twofold division is the sensual/spiritual dichotomy, which as *projection* reflects how men perceive women, rather than how women perceive, or are in themselves. The last entity I would consider myself to be (or want to be seen as), for instance, is Wolff's version of 'medium', owing to its colloquial connotation as a psychic channeller of deceased spirits. I'm not implying that you're determined to slot me into this category. Although if Wolff's cap fits (me), however uncomfortably, I prefer the term *mediatrix,* if this is taken to mean 'one who acts as a creative bridge to the collective unconscious'.

Toni Wolff, for instance, allowed herself to become for Jung the personification of the anima as the collective unconscious, a challenge which took enormous courage, strength and dedication on her and, needless to say, Jung's wife Emma's part. As far as the other types go, being a 'mother' is not confined to its biological expression, as I have well and truly learned through my experience with loving children, and with adopting nurturing roles in general. My song on my album *Dancer,* 'Lady of Sylvairen', was written for a child I loved and still love beyond measure, though she's now a happily married woman.

Your connection of the flower writing/sorting section of my Dream with *The Black Grail* is fascinating, to say the least. To further unveil the tapestry — and since you asked about my fiction — I've enclosed extracts from a science fantasy novel, *An Era in Anddemar,* not for their literary merit, the lack of which I hope you'll be gracious enough to overlook, but rather because it's also a personal mythology which has developed over many years. In *An Era in Anddemar* I identify with each face of the galaxy's threefold Goddess; with Celendien, the central figure (whom as you know I dreamed of being), and with two of her daughters: the goddess Nhaiarva, a Nature Guardian/Mother and the goddess Starwing, a Fiorinda-like, ethereal Mediatrix to 'The Dreaming' of Anddemar. I hasten to add that no 'amazons' have barged in yet, probably because I'm too gentle a soul to relate to this overtly masculinised energy.

My *Anddemar* myth throws some light on my relation to the (masculine archetype of) the *animus,* hence indirectly reflects how this has played out in my past relationships with men. I've always been drawn to men who were animus projections that reminded me of my father — with whom I have an incredibly close relationship – in one way or another. You, on the other hand, are the first man I've connected with emotionally who is the exact opposite of my ideal animus figure, the latter appearing in *Anddemar* as the 'dark knight'. It dawned on me only recently, given that this now seems obvious, that 'dark knight' is the antithesis of you as 'Daystar', or 'Day' (which I've been calling you intuitively for months).

But this is where it gets really interesting: if I exist (as Darkbloom) in your mythology of *The Black Grail*, you, in turn, have appeared as a character in *Anddemar,* something I realised only comparatively recently, namely as the powerful, wise Trickster Terragian, for whom, significantly, the 'dark knight' has immense love and respect. Of course I know you to be far more – and in other ways far less – than this archetypal figure, since one must never completely identify with an archetype (= inflation), nor allow the ego to be subsumed by it (= psychosis, usually.) A core principle of Jungian psychology is never to constrain life to fit any theory, no matter how convenient, or 'right' it may seem.

What is significant is that when Terragian appears on the scene, he completely upsets the applecart with feats of juggling, cryptic questioning and kaleidoscopic revelry, and causes the perspective of the narrative to subvert itself by reverting to its opposite, at which point I abandoned the whole thing (about two years ago.) Not the end of the story, however, since as Jung makes clear, if we fail to deal with a challenge on one level (e.g. inwardly), it will come at us from another angle, often as outer destiny.

Your mention of Eros is uncanny, again in a good way, and your comments about Psyche's deserved punishment were incisive, since (don't laugh) a few days before receiving your letter I dreamed of you as Eros, complete with one of those Greek helmets that have wings at their sides! The thing was, your eyes were like infinitely reflecting mirrors – the effect you get when two mirrors face one another — such that I could see in them countless reflections of myself. Where will it all end, I thought? Not surprisingly, facing mirrors often means confronting the unconscious shadow. The relevant truth is, I didn't react at all well to certain aspects of your letter and it took me awhile to deal with these aroused defensive emotions and attitudes, which had been triggered by an aversion to my own shadow, which you have already prompted me to face.

Getting back to our mythologies: the 'dark knight', like yours truly, is intense, dark, brooding, obsessive, and as such could do with a good deal of lightening up. Starwing often takes him at night through the Dreaming to other planets or regions of the galaxy. Aaivan, who appears as a creative animus in the guise of ancient, cosmic Eros, is (also) Jung's *puer aeternus*, the Divine Child, who guides the feminine psyche (as Psyche) toward understanding the deep mysteries of love. The characters and storyline of *Anddemar* were envisioned well before I encountered Jung, however, which is why I asked you some time ago whether your archetypal constructs in *The Black Grail* were consciously adapted from Jung, or arose spontaneously, or both.

But the synchronicities keep multiplying: in connection with your 'Darkbloom' or 'Flowers of Evening', Starwing's true name, 'Naudicea', means 'nocturnal white orchid', and she is seen (in the passage I sent you) gathering flowers that bloom in the evening. Funny how flowers keep popping up (dreadful pun). The later 'Adagio' chapter of *Anddemar* again involves Sir Jaide and Starwing and their discussions about their shared quest to deal with the 'Greyness' that is the enemy of both light and dark. Also, in view of my Dream of us as rapidly interweaving stars, note J and S's metaphoric 'orbit of shared distance and entwinement'. You'll probably wince at the clumsily Eddisonish prose style, unless you like that sort of thing, which I do; it's quite deliberate, since later on it's subverted by the Trickster. And speaking of caps fitting uncomfortably or not, Terragian sometimes wears a draping, rainbow-patchwork beret which is topped by an ornament resembling a purple strawberry.

On to other matters: I'm truly sorry to hear of your persistent trouble with headaches and wish there was something I could do to help, though I'm relieved to hear that they've subsided since the advent of your new stove. If only all your damned medical problems would disappear for good! I know this sounds a bit mediumish, but I have a nifty tiger iron massage wand that might help you here, even though you'd probably view this as a suspiciously New Age-like treatment.

I'm glad to hear about your recent delving into Jung. From what I recall, though, I disliked Anthony Stevens' book on archetypes, since he reductively fails to appreciate that the archetype is — in Jung's view at least — transpersonal and transcendent, numinous and emotional, not merely physiological. There are better books around on archetypes, for example Marie-Louise von Franz's *Projection and Re-Collection in Jungian Psychology,* which I'll loan you when I see you, if you're interested; though of course one can't go past Jung's key *CW* volumes, especially 'Aion', 'Mysterium Coniunctionis' and 'The Archetypes and the Collective Unconscious'.

Your and Rory's *Valencies* is a delightful read and reminds me a bit of some of PKD's straight fiction; and your hilarious 'Nightingsnail Canto' wonderfully retains the spirit of the original. Keats, who had an offbeat sense of humour, would have loved it, I'm sure. Now I'm about to start in earnest on *Reading By Starlight,* so I hope to be able to discuss it with you when I see you. My talk on the ABC was nothing spectacular, by the way, merely a live interview to promote my forthcoming sf course for the Uni of Adelaide.

I certainly look forward to seeing you. And don't worry, when I suggested the possibility of a 'retreat', I wasn't suggesting anything so masochistic as hiking. No, never fear, sloth, though I prefer the Keatsian euphemism 'diligent Indolence', is ever the name of the main game with me. What I had in view, rather, was an old-fashioned, tastefully furnished, renovated chapel, a quaint little hideaway and just the sort of place for getting-to-know-someone-better in. I wondered if you might be keen to share a few restful days there, perhaps with some good music, books, and a hamper full of delectable goodies. It also has a nifty skylight for viewing the stars, as well as deer, sheep and ducks wandering about outside.

Blessings (and flowers) in abundance

26 October 1994

Dear Damien

I'm glad you didn't mind being loosely identified with my Trickster figure, even to the extent of endorsing his millinery eccentricities. Why, then, should I have been annoyed at being seen as Wolff's 'medium'? To tell the truth, I regretted sending my last letter to you and apologise for its guardedness and wildly Jungian speculations. If I'm a secretive soul, it's to some extent a temperamental quirk, perhaps as the necessary 'shadow' of your commendable openness, though probably sparked as well by neurotic fears of rejection (based on past hurts), and other irrational defences. If it's any consolation, I'm far less secretive than I used to be and, to quote The Beatles, 'it's getting better all the time'. I assure you it also has nothing to do with intentional dishonesty, or lack of trust in you.

Anyway, given the sensitivity of your response to my puerile peevishness, I'm ashamed that I hinted at being 'upset' by whatever it was I balked at. My balk is worse than your bite. I have no intention of holding you responsible for any trivial, or defensive reactions that any of your innocent remarks might have triggered. My shadow is my problem, not anyone else's, and rest assured that the matter has been laid to rest. I'm sorry, then, if I caused you any concern, given that I've only ever felt from you kindness, acceptance — even in the face of your often radically opposing stance — patience and tolerance, so I don't intend to unload onto you any of my personal crap.

Furthermore, I assure you I've never yet 'run screaming with anger' from a room, nor am I ever likely to; it's just not my style. I prefer more subtle, good-humoured and kind responses. Besides, why on earth should anything you say anger me? On the contrary, I thrive off of your opposing perspectives in that, as I've implied, they are the challenge I need and secretly crave in order to counterbalance my own biases. Where would the mutual growth and reward be otherwise?

All that I know of you thus far, including the odd bouts of surly grouchiness, I find personally endearing. In comparison, our enjoyable speculations over the nature of reality are comparatively impersonal. Absolute truth, if it exists, is not a private concern to be jealously defended, but rather an ongoing quest which demands ruthless honesty and detachment, yet is perhaps more enriching when shared. Since your vantage point is usually antithetical to my own, together we might discover (while gazing at the stars) a resolving synthesis beyond our personal egos. Far from being angered by your comments on *Anddemar*, then, I feel honoured to receive some insightful and much needed criticism from a writer of your stature.

As it happens, I'd already arrived at the same conclusions as yours, namely that the whole thing is artificially one-sided and lacking, as you note, a sense of 'the business of life', which is why I abandoned it yet also hit on the idea of deliberately subverting this bias later on. But would this tactic work as a literary device? I'm not sure, since I can't think of any successful precedents. And as you succinctly put it, 'nectar's fine but toast and crumbs helps'. Precisely, which is why I admire and have learned so much from the more down-to-earth wholesomeness of your writing. Still, I wouldn't mind having another go at *Anddemar* at some stage, with your suggested improvements in view, and I certainly appreciate your kind offer to help with a tentative submission to HarperCollins.

I was fascinated to hear about your venturing into the lions' den of the teaching arena. My sf course at the Uni of Adelaide began this week and, I'm relieved to say, got an enthusiastic audience response. I've got about 20 students and kicked off with a discussion of genre definitions, origins, and the meanings and relevance of 'myth' and 'science' to sf. You'd probably be horrified at the sorts of things I'm aiming to discuss later on: Jung, archetypes, Tricksters, transcendence.... Hopefully not to your annoyance, I've got *The Dreaming Dragons, The Black Grail* and *The Sea's Furthest End* on the recommended reading list. Next week I'm focussing on 60s writers: Zelazny, Le Guin, Delany, Silverberg and Ballard. I'm sure your English Dept lecture wasn't the disaster you made it out to be; you probably just copped the usual apathetic first years' response (to everything), which not even your attempted Trickster routine would have assuaged. Incidentally, can you believe that some of my students were even bored by *Star Trek*? The effrontery of it!

A radio adaptation of *Reading By Starlight* sounds like a worthwhile venture. As for the book itself, I'm overwhelmed (as usual) by your eloquent brilliance and had to do my usual share of running to the dictionary. I found your discussion of Terry Dowling's work particularly illuminating and would like to quote some of it in my course. Even though I don't personally relate as much as you do to the assumed centrality of semiotics and linguistic tropes in sf, I appreciate your respect for the inventiveness and subversiveness of language in the genre. I also enjoyed your imaginative proposal that 'genre is a negotiated territory in narrative phase space'; but the finest sentence in the book is on p. 14: 'Ideas tumble about the page like performing animals, like humans infected by diseases of information'. Before I forget, I haven't yet managed to get hold of your book on parapsychology, so is there any chance you could bring over a copy for me to read while you're here?

I've just finished Dann and Haldeman's *High Steel,* which I found engrossing, partly because it confirmed certain insights I've had about holistic evolutionary trends in cosmogonic mythogenesis. One focus of the book, which concerns a Red Indian character as the focal observer, thus mythic dreamer and creator of a universe, reminded me of your Dayton in *Sea,* while the epiphanic merging of technology and human consciousness seemed similar to the way your Soul Core was experienced in *The Dreaming Dragons*. I've also just read Zelazny's *The Dream Master,* which is pretty Jungian, and Greg Bear's *The Infinity Concerto,* which doesn't fit comfortably into any genre.

We both seem to mean different things by 'transcendent' and 'archetype'. Jung, for instance, uses the term 'transcendent function' in reference to the power of the uniting symbol to effect a change in attitude, by bridging the conscious and unconscious. Your connection of archetypes with collective grammatical structures may be valid, but it assumes that the nature of the unconscious is, as Lacan believes it to be, linguistic. Also, he fails to differentiate between the personal and collective strata. The nature of dreams, myths, symbols, alchemy and visions suggests that the linguistic hypothesis is inadequate, since dreams and suchlike are all transrational modes of apperception. You ask: 'Why should the form constants of our unconscious cognition and feeling have a different kind of source?' My reply is: why shouldn't they? Of course 'biologising' isn't reductive if it's true; but what if it isn't?

As I understand it, the transcendent nature of archetypes arises from the psyche-matter polar nature of the collective unconscious, which is a self-affirming unitary reality that is mediated to itself. From this perspective the notion of a 'transcendental signifier', for instance, is nonsense, since the sign-signifier pairing is a linguistic dualism arising from the conscious attempt to inscribe meaning within linguistic bounds. One doesn't, or can't 'project the inner world into the outer' from within the lived reality of a transcendental substratum in which exists no distinction between inner and outer; hence synchronistic phenomena are the meaningful coincidence of 'inner' and 'outer' events, precipitated by the activation of archetypes. Hmm, looks like we could be in for some fascinating discussions here, so thank the gods we have a common yearning to yield to 'awe and numinosity and ravishing music and ravishing'.

Your casual mention of your 'crippled soul' is an uncanny reminder of one ingredient of my Dream of us which I haven't yet disclosed to you, and would only do so in person. I can say that it was the most vivid and disturbing 'scene' in the entire Dream. And why should you, of all people, be craving 'respectability' when you've earned it a thousand times over?

What a dreary synchronicity this time, you having to visit the dentist and me having just returned from one when I found your letter. I've always maintained that dentists' lairs should be labelled — in honour of Pope (or was it Dryden?) — 'The Abode of Dullness'. Anyway, I hope whatever surgery you needed wasn't too drastic. It's all a part of corporeal ruin, I suppose. And as I've said repeatedly, I certainly look forward to seeing you. There's only so much that can be achieved through writing letters, as enjoyable as it is; personal communion allows for more finely-tuned and immediate responses.

Are you aware, by the way, that the Australian F1 Grand Prix is on again from 3–6 November? I have a nauseous knot in my stomach just thinking about it, after having met that wonderful soul Ayrton Senna at the last Grand Prix, and then in some sense being with him when he tragically died. I'm in tears recalling it and dread the heart-wrenching emotion that the roar of those F1 engines will bring on.

T has acquired several dozen of an exquisite French peach champagne, so I might take the opportunity to acquire a couple of bottles for our private consumption at the skylighted chapel. For the gods' sake don't break your leg, or something else while boarding the plane. Meanwhile, I'll have a few days to stock my larder and fridge with incredible edibles. I've been searching for purple strawberries, to no avail.

Love and lunacy

23 November 1994

Dear Damien

Thanks so much for the loan of the enclosed enjoyable read, which I thought I'd best return pronto in case you need to consult your annotations in the near future. Sadly, as you'll note, the binding has reached disintegration mode, in spite of my sensitive handling of the book. Strange how, in contrast, one's hundred year-old volumes remain intact. I must say I'm in awe of the huge amount of time and effort you must have put into such a solid and entertaining bout of research. Let's hope it receives the follow-up and serious attention it deserves, perhaps through being studied by interested Psychology departments. (I think I mentioned that Adelaide Uni used to do ESP experiments.) I enjoyed the witty subheadings and comments, and your discussion of quantum phenomena out-Hawkings Paul Davies, whom I observed wandering about the campus a few days ago.

Well, did you find your roof blown off when you returned home? I hope so, given that, as I recall, you hoped it would be. I'm also hopeful that the irksome confines of my cramped couch haven't aggravated your sense of corporeal ruin, not that I detected much evidence of the latter.

It's business as usual here. A few days back I was voted in as the new President of the SA Mythopoeic Society, which ironically translates into my having to do less work than I've thus far done to keep the whole thing afloat for the past three years or so. T announced at the same meeting that the theme for the Darwin Mythopoeic Conference (next July) will be 'the Grotesque'. Hmm. I wonder if that's why he thought of inviting you along as guest speaker? (Just kidding.) We also decided that since we've amassed excess funds, we can afford to invite over a few interstate speakers next year. Would you care to be flown over as one of them? Let me know if you're interested and I'll put forward the idea to the Committee.

My folks took off for a Tasmania holiday last Thursday. In fact, I'm pretty sure they were on your flight out of town, so I've entrenched myself at their place in (to quote you) 'benediction of the quotidian', amidst the modest luxuries of air-conditioning, gas fires, a decent garden for pottering and potting in, a capacious bath for luxuriating in and, most importantly, a piano to singalong with. I've been doing a fair amount of reading — though I'll never match your twelve hour a day stints — including *Neuromancer* (again).

I admit to acquiring an increasing fascination with cyberpunk as a self-consciously literary form. It intrigues me how it's able to invert the expansiveness and sometimes false optimism of traditional quest tropes, for example, Gibson's bizarre, quasi-mythic 'Villa Straylight', a high-tech kind of ceremonial construct, patterned like a circuited mandala and folded into a monetary 'seamless universe of self'. Pondering the obscure purpose of such alien modes of existence is, I find, quite seductive. I've also been enjoying your discussion (in *Reading By Starlight*) of Delany's reinvention of mythic forms, a task in which you have succeeded admirably.

Last night at my sf course, I discussed *Blade Runner*, cyberpunk, and Arthur C. Clarke in the context of utopian and dystopian visions. I also handed out extracts from *The Dreaming Dragons* and *The Sea's Furthest End*, and offered condolences to the students who'd missed hearing you speak last week. Next week I'll probably discuss PKD and his Gnostic pink-beam visions.

Have you made progress with *The White Abacus*? Your ideas for it sounded commendably ambitious, and only a writer of your calibre could pull off such a challenge. I must say I was grieved to hear you express such low esteem for your writing thus far, given that I see in it the rare combination of a sensitivity to life, power, passion and brilliance. I sense that you've not yet done your best work, which, I suggest, might well depend on a certain Dreamed right hand being restored to wholeness. But my wish is for all your inner wounds to become healed, as mine have begun to be through knowing you. For now, I hope to goodness that your headaches are things of the past and that your injured toe has resumed normal functioning. I'm about to start reading George Turner's *Beloved Son*, so it's time to brew a fresh pot of coffee.

Take care, Dayananda.

1 December 1994

Dear Damien

I always enjoy being in Melbourne, so whenever you feel up to a visit, let me know and I'll zap on over.

As I mentioned, the feeling-tone of my Dream of us, like its visual dimension was particularly clear. In the Dream the barrier between us arose not from ideological differences, but from your inner conflict between the legitimate pride that goes with self-respect and self-reliance, and your deeper, rejected need for the healing of certain deep wounds related to your past. No doubt, though, you're by now sick and tired of hearing about said Dream, so after describing what follows, I'll make every effort not to mention it again. In one part of the Dream you were standing alone, unable to use either arm, in a kind of emotional paralysis, and I could neither touch nor draw close to you; it was, as well as I can recall, in the scene which followed that you held up your badly burnt hand. I remain haunted by that Dream, saddened and stunned by its prophetic accuracy.

The truth is, if you hadn't made your tell-tale comment about seeking the Perfect Other, all this would probably have remained unsaid, but since you did make it I felt it would be dishonest and irresponsible of me not to respond by sharing how I see the matter. The gods know I have no wish to depress, or disturb you, but neither do I wish to see you remain trapped through clinging to an illusion which can never bring you the healing and contentment you need and deserve.

What I have already learned from you is too deep to be put into words, so perhaps I can shed some light, however faint, on a field in which I have faced the most difficult challenges of my life. In Robert Johnson's book, Tristan, by seeking the 'Perfect Other' in an outer person ('Iseult the Fair') rather than as the inner mediatrix she needs to be, fails to appreciate the genuine love which, in the person of 'Iseult of the Earth', is all the time staring him in the face. It takes immense courage for a man to come to terms with the psychological implications of this deceptively simple book, but if you're serious about your quest for the feminine, and I sense you are, it might be worth your attention.

As for me, I no longer subscribe to the false ideal of a 'perfect other', having at last realised that the inner masculine animus can only ever be a mediator to truth, to the wonder of the Cosmos and the sense of the divine. Nor do I have a desire, or need to be romantically idealised as an anima figure. I'm too individuated to be a plausible candidate for that role anyway. My outer quest for the animus was the search for my father, but now I've finally come to love — rather than merely be in love with — a man who's not an animus figure. As I've said before, you're the exact opposite of one. For me, then, the spell appears to have been broken and I'm grateful that it is less likely to ever entrap me again. Could it be, though, that you're still seeking outwardly, instead of within, the unattainable perfection of your anima? Your comments about seeking your mother, perhaps in the same way that I for so long sought my father, hinted that this might be the case.

Johnson's book teases out the distinction between the inwardness of 'romance', as one's relationship with the contrasexual archetype, and the outwardness of true relatedness, as that which develops only between two individuated selves. What I suspected might happen when you came over here is precisely what did unfold. Goodness, do you think I hoped you would fall in love with me? I assure you I shall continue to hope for far more — and in another sense far less — than this; less because no mortal woman can compete with a goddess as the longed for Perfect Other of a man's soul-image; more because, like you, I would prefer to be loved for myself, since I happen to feel she is, for all her imperfections, a likeable and loveable person.

The warning signals were certainly becoming evident in your letters: allusions to me in connection with the 'goddess' as your 'Flowers of Evening' (the equivalent of 'Iseult the Fair') — classic anima projection stuff. Your casual remark about 'the wistful dream of the Perfect Other' hints at false expectations you perhaps had of whatever time we'd spend together. Indeed, after you'd gone, though I suppose it was some time before, I was left with the gut feeling that by failing to live up to a perhaps idealised, romantic image you'd concocted of me, I was an inevitable disappointment to you, being as I am a mere human being, as you are.

Of course I, too, had fabricated — on the basis of your letters and published works — an image, and I wondered how the real you would compare. My reaction, though, was far from disappointment, because I knew in advance that the image was bound to be tainted with faint echoes of my abandoned father-image quest. Now, instead of clinging to a distorted picture of you, I care deeply for the man himself, warts and all, for although you cling to a need to prove your intellectual worth to others, I value and have immense affection for you in spite of your brilliance, not because of it, and I have no regrets that it is so. But dear me, I don't wish to sound melodramatic, or gloomy, since I assure you I'm far from feeling such emotions. I enjoyed the time I spent with you, and I confess to missing you deeply. As well, touching and being touched by you was, for me, at least, a comforting and pleasurably therapeutic experience, which I, too, hope we shall share again.

I've had the gall to enclose the Johnson volume, since I vaguely recall you mentioning that someone had advised you to read it. I can assure you I won't be offended if, instead, you trade it in at the local Book Exchange for something you'd rather have. But I'll add that I don't need the book back because, dare I say, I've well and truly learned — through past disappointments and present insights into 'love' — its complementary feminine lessons, although few of us, it seems, ever emerge from the labyrinths of projection-making. The distinction the book makes between genuine love and romantic idealisations that are doomed to disappointment, focuses on the illusions of 'in-loveness' versus the underrated simplicities of 'love'. After all, one needs to pass and see through 'dis-illusionment' before the humble opacity of the real can be embraced for the lasting treasures of companionship it offers.

Where there's shared trust and affection, relationships thrive on the creative challenge of the complementary Other. Thus whereas you see an obstacle in our differing stances — not that mine have ever been inflexible — I see instead a healthy tension of opposites grounded in mutual respect, as was symbolised by the 'binary star' opening image in my Dream of us. I suppose this is why I said I was sadder for you than I was for myself; sad because for all your brilliance and integrity, you continue to deny yourself the kind of love which is the true mystery of the feminine principle, compared to the dramatics and Maya of the anima, the 'Eros' whom Jung describes as the 'father-mother of all higher consciousness'. But I don't want to sound like a proselytiser; deep in your heart you no doubt already know these truths. And as for what we don't yet understand, I'm sure you'll agree that life, like the best sf, habitually undermines our certainties.

My love always

6 December 1994

Dear Almost Famous Skiffy Scribbler

We keep crossing letters. What, aside from the obviousness of great minds thinking alike, could it mean? A spin/anti-spin synchronisation of quantum non-locality?

When I turned up a bit early at the last night of the sf course last Tuesday, a couple of students were sitting outside, absorbed in reading *The Sea's Furthest End.* Not surprisingly, on seeing me they ventured to extol its brilliance, and one of them avidly praised the credibility of the leading characters, with whom she totally empathised. Yes, yes, I said. Now, have you read his other stuff (which I proceeded to list, describe, and similarly extol). Following that evening's session I went for coffee with a few of the women I'd gotten to know reasonably well, all of whom seemed more enthused than the guys were about the weird insights I've been putting forward. They were all well-versed in the field, too; one had been reading gutsy sf solidly for twenty years, so was way ahead of me. The previous week, one guy complained that we hadn't been talking enough about 'science' and so missed this final session, in which science is all we did talk about, by not turning up.

I'm glad to hear that *The Architecture of Babel* is getting the rave reviews it deserves. If your brother sends you the *Sydney Morning Herald* version, I wouldn't mind a copy. All your hassling about with *Theory and Its Discontents* sounds boring, though. I hate to say it, but La Trobe's financial dithering sounds suspiciously like a smokescreen for a hidden excuse for delay. I hope that's not the case; I guess you're used to dealing with apathetic publishers by now, but their apparent glib indifference, if not outright rudeness, strikes me as deplorable.

Strange goings at the final Mythopoeic meeting for the year: T presented a highly animated, mildly grotesque rendering of a fairy-tale about some 'chronologically advanced' goats and a scheming troll, which he preceded with a lengthy explanation of why the traditional 'Fat Boys' of many a Christmas tale should — in order to be politically correct — be known as 'Horizontally Enhanced Persons'. Alas, maybe your mind-melting visit to his home finally pushed him over the edge. Still, his wife made up for the ordeal of this weird interlude by providing some tasty, home-made mince pies; and at least some of the questions in the traditional end-of-year quiz were answerable. While mingling for supper, I casually shared with a couple of Committee members my suggestion that we invite you over next year. Having downed a few ports, they thought this would be a superb plan. We've already got someone lined up for February, so how about mid-March?

I've just sent off a paper on the psychological significance of the Grail in some Arthurian literature, for possible inclusion in an anthology being edited by Kath Filmer (founder of the Mythopoeic Literature Society) at Queensland UP. I've also received a couple of 'not interested' replies from publishers regarding my Keats book, but have yet to hear from a few others. Thanks for offering to do some sample editing of my long-winded thesis style; I assure you I'm grateful and herewith enclose some rambling excepts for your perusal.

I found your 'Foundation' stuff revealing, especially the bits about your childhood and early pseudo-hippie days at Uni. It struck me as idiotic that in his review K should admit that *Sea* inwardly 'connects', then complains that it 'fails to add up to a simple reading', a statement obliquely condoning the lack of challenging ideas that in turn feeds mental lethargy. Gee, and I always thought sf was meant to be provocative. So you subvert the reader's expectations. Why should it be considered remotely 'odd' for you, of all writers, to do precisely that? And K makes it sound as if it's all been achieved accidentally rather than intentionally.

We're having a heat-wave here, which is synchronising well with my reading of the *Helliconia* novels. I'm about to start the second ('Summer'), having just finished the first ('Spring'), which, judging (wrongly) from the 4-winged reptilian worm on the cover, was not what I expected. Although you thought I'd probably like this series, I'm finding it a bit staid, predictable and Earthbound for my more adventurous taste, though I admire anyone who can convincingly sustain a vision on so vast a scale; and I revel in the elegant prose, from which I could learn a thing or two. I've also just got hold of Zindell's *Neverness* through an interlibrary loan.

How are you planning to spend (or not spend) Christmas? I wish it would either go away, or return to its original intent as a celebration of the birth of Christ. The best one I ever spent was a couple of years ago, when I zoomed off on a jet to glow-worm caved, glaciered New Zealand, surely the most beautiful country in the world.

Love

14 December 1994

Dear Damien

I've just come back from a several-day jaunt (not à la Bester, unfortunately) to the Cape Jervis region, since I thought I'd go loony if I didn't get out of town for a while and hence did so in the company of a close pal, a single mum whose kids were away for the week. As a result of this revitalising spree, spent for the most in paddling along beaches and foraging among rock pools, I'm now poised to catch up with your past few letters.

In your rejoinder to my recent party-pooping letter sent with the Johnson book, I got the impression that you were venting a lot of anger against life, the universe, everything, so I thought I'd best let you cool off a bit. Come to think of it, I cooled off, too, during my seaside adventure. But returning to your letters, I'm glad you weren't too annoyed by the Johnson book; your response was in fact milder than I expected it would be. To begin with, I must say I'm relieved to hear that I'm not a failed anima figure. I've played that dismal role too many times, and I hope you'll forgive me for underestimating you by implying that you're more of a romantic idealist than I am. As you suggest, the reverse is all too likely to be true, which would make you, not surprisingly perhaps, closer to being a successfully individuated person than I am. You're wrong to assume that I consider myself to be a prime example of the latter; alas, very few ever get that far along the bumpy road to enlightenment. All I meant was that since the archetype is the *possibility* of form, a lack of clear character facilitates another person's projection of said archetype into a ready-made, vacant psychic space. Hence dumb bimbos, for instance, make ideal targets for anima projections, not that I was conjecturing such crassness to be coming from you. Rather, I thought that in your case it might be an instance of the more generalised 'projection onto a relatively unknown'.

Still, I enjoyed your discussion of the bits Johnson fails to take note of, or conveniently ignores, and it's not surprising that you shrewdly pinpoint a distinctive quirk of many intuitive introverts, namely, their tendency to gather evidence selectively in support of absolute ideas, rather than allow ideas to emerge from and be shaped by available facts and competing paradigms. Since you're a more extraverted thinker than I am, you understandably find this intuitive bias irksome, but then intuitives think the same of fact-oriented perception. Nonetheless, your valid questions and alternative reading of the Tristan myth convincingly contest Johnson's more blinker-visioned view. Hey, why not write a book about it? You don't, though, invalidate his central psychological premise. To put it plainly, there's too much evidence in daily life that the projection business is alive and well, thanks in part to its reinforcement in Hollywood 'myths', Mills and Boon novels, 'Days of Our Lives', and other escapist trivia. Plus one becomes painfully aware of these psychological games when on the receiving end of them.

It's significant that you should ask why Hindus don't have a problem with anima and animus projections. A few years back Johnson devoted an entire talk at the Adelaide Jung Society to this phenomenon. The basic principle at work is that although the archetype is universal, its social manifestation varies from culture to culture in accord with the nature of the cultural shadow. Thus if projection is the outer search for the inner divinity of the self, since sexuality is consciously repressed and excluded (as the shadow) from the Western God-image, it's unconsciously projected in a negative form elsewhere, namely as part of the world/flesh/Devil complex (cf. flesh-hating Catholics), in opposition to commendably sexless femininity, exemplified by the Virgin Mary, which was secularly epitomised by the medieval cult of Courtly Love. Since the Hindus have a different collective shadow, their gods, on the other hand, are consciously reconciled to sexuality, as is evident in the erotic nature of much of their religious symbolism; so they don't tend to project erotic archetypes onto people, at least to the pathological extent that Westerners do.

But as you surmised in your tirade against Johnson and New Agers, my main concern for you is the inner healing you see yourself in need of. Don't worry, I know all about your 'hyper-vigilance'. I experienced it on July 3, remember, in — yes, you guessed it — that precognitive Dream. At the risk of being a bore, I'll remind you that my awareness of your 'emotional paralysis' and need for healing did not, as you suggest it did, derive to any extent from stories you, or anyone, have told me. I barely knew you at the time of that Dream, since I'd only spoken to you for ten minutes or so, and that, as I recall, was about quantum physics. Why else would I have remained stunned and puzzled about it all for weeks thereafter, until I worked up the guts to write to you? When you held up your burnt hand in that Dream, your response was obviously ambiguous, as if you were saying symbolically, 'I want you to see this, but keep your distance'. One's rejected shadow often appears as symbolically crippled, or wounded, hence my Dream perhaps had a dual significance in being about my own inner condition, as well as about you.

The 'burnt hand' motif cropped up in the film *The Fisher King*, which I saw for the first time a few weeks back. The story is that the Fisher King, who is perpetually wounded, saw the Grail in a fire and, believing it would bring him power and recognition, reached in to take it and was consequently burnt. He needed to learn, in other words, that the Grail must be used for the healing of others, not for oneself only. As you've suggested before, you have this gift of healing. The truth is, you are a kind, gentle, considerate, sensitive, likeable, loveable and understanding man, and no, I don't think that saying so, after having perceived and experienced these qualities, is a romantic over-valuation. Besides, only someone who is deeply sensitive would feel a need to put up a self-defensive shield as strong as yours. In fact, the emotional barrier you project, in terms of non-verbal cues, is quite formidable. And just as through the false security of reason you cut yourself off from the possibility of *gnosis* (as intuitive knowledge of the heart), so with the kind of self-protection you adopt you shield yourself from pain and disappointment, but also deny yourself the possibility of their opposites.

Furthermore, if I'm guilty (as you claim I am) of over-valuing you and your writing, perhaps you'll concede that the inverse may be equally true in your under-valuation of the same. Maybe to balance the scales we both need to move a bit in the opposite direction. Perhaps we each have strengths where the other is weak. Since you're no more screwed up a person than I am, that is, if we're both deficient as well as proficient in complementary ways, maybe we can help heal one another's wounded areas. I realise, of course, that this all might sound simplistic to a mind of your profundity and astuteness, but then perhaps that's why the Neoplatonists called the One 'the Simple', a synonym of Truth as that which is indivisible, versus the 'dis-ease' of wounded fragmentation.

I'll go even further out on the same limb by suggesting that as long as you reject the healing which being loved can offer, you reinforce the self-loathing which you are in reality free to renounce at any time; that is, unless you secretly believe the Catholic dogma that we're all wretched scum. You mention the possibility of bravely taking the plunge by turning for help to possible experts in the field, but maybe — I don't know — the solution is simpler than that, perhaps even somewhere along Johnson's unsophisticated lines. I'm neither a guru nor a trained therapist, but I do know that I was deeply moved by that precognitive Dream, and I'd dearly like to be of some help to you in finding whatever healing you need. Neither do I know a great deal about your past, only what I've read and what you've told me, but I can assure you that I, too, have been deeply hurt by being abandoned for bimbo-ish anima figures, and it amazes me that I haven't turned into a ranting, macho feminist in response.

For some perverse reason I've gone in the opposite direction. I guess I've been subsumed by the archetype of the 'Wounded

Healer', and I recognise in you, too, this gift, such that I would love to see, for your sake, your creative momentum shift from the need to prove your worth toward more compassionate aims. But of course the love of others begins with the love of oneself, and the love of oneself must include a recognition that one is loveable. Alright, I know I'm drifting close to proselytising here, and I'm also aware that your tendency might be to react cynically, but then isn't cynicism the most effective mode of defence against the presumed inevitability, rather than possibility, of being hurt?

On a more detached front, your sincerity and intellectual rigour in questioning what you regard as spurious holistic revelations are qualities which I seek to emulate — and I'm not idealising you here either. Nevertheless, to paraphrase Jung, the transrational fullness of life has taught me never to dismiss anything, even when it undermines our beliefs, or is otherwise inexplicable. We can never be certain that our inner compass is reliable, but certainty doesn't lead to understanding, which requires love and humility. In my experience, some insights arise only through apparently foolish leaps of faith, at the end of which certainty sometimes arises from uncertainty, and sometimes vice versa. All in all, no-one has disrupted my smug complacencies and false certainties to the extent you have, and I don't mind if you derive some macabre amusement from it.

I don't know about there being 'one great truth', Darwinian or otherwise. As you know, I'm always suspicious of unilateralism, since the one great truth is that life is a great paradox, which as such thrives on the creative tension of opposing energies, perfectly symbolised by the Dance of Shiva and the yin/yang symbol of Tao. Randomness may in certain instances be the overriding truth, but then its complement emerges at other times, for instance in the spontaneous growths of order in different fluid systems. Hence the ambivalent self, whose existence you deny, is not primarily a premise, or a notion; it is, at heart, an instinctive expression of the unity and multiplicity of Tao. Hence while our beliefs are one-sided ego constructs, the self as a kaleidoscopic unity of multiple identities, is a perpetual permutation which alternately centres and de-centres itself. Surrendering unity and surrendering to it are thus two sides of the same coin, which, in a nutshell, is what the dance of individuation involves. I've also learned from experience that our hypothetical mid-point, the antinomial self, has a purpose distinct from the ego's bias, in that it strives instead for wholeness, through bridging all modes of 'dis-eased' one-sidedness. Hence by relinquishing a narcissistic ideal – bearing in view that self-loathing and self-aggrandisement are two sides of the same psychic coin – one can become open to the vaster spectrum of life's boundless potential.

In my own mostly alone, though never lonely experience, life has ruthlessly thrown what I need, rather than what I've wished for, into my path, a thus far bizarre quest which has unfolded as if it's had some mythic, Grail-directed purpose of its own, at least in so far as I perceive certain recurring themes and challenges weaving through it. Of course there's a risky kind of madness in allowing this to happen, a sense of handing over the reins to something – someone? – that knows more than I am consciously aware of. And this unseen charioteer, if she exists, is hopefully a wiser aspect of myself.

But if you will settle only for rational explanations, you will never be convinced of the reality of a mysterious core self, nor of the archetypes that orbit it. No-one who has been overwhelmed by one or more archetypes actually goes looking for them. (Have you come across Charles Williams' spiritual thriller *The Place of the Lion*?) No, one is more likely to run away, although some of us, it seems, are doomed to be pounced upon. As Jung always stressed, as far as archetypes, including the self, are concerned, we begin with an experience, not a theory. For me, as I've mentioned before, the self in the guise of an imploding singularity repeatedly overwhelmed me as a child. It was only much later that its comparatively benevolent face manifested, when — visually and emotionally, in the symbolic guise of visions of mandalas and the 'inner marriage' — a spontaneous, compensating order imposed itself on an emotionally overloaded inner crisis, which was channelled into my dreadful novel, *The Cross Connection.* And all this happened before I'd heard of Jung.

All this aside, keep in view when you deny the 'perennial philosophy' that you're talking about an intuition that's persisted for thousands of years, around 5000 in the case of the *I Ching,* in comparison with the puny infancy of our hubristic paradigm of Western science which, ironically, is shifting back toward holism, though I know you'd disagree with this. Surely the sheer tenacity of gnosis as heart-centred intuition makes it at least worthy of consideration, unless you're willing to claim that the likes of Confucius, Lao-tse, Plato, Bohr, Pauli, Jung, Kant, Spinoza, not to mention PKD, Le Guin, Ballard — and yours truly — are all complete idiots. I respect and have learned much from your views, and I admire the personal integrity which energises them; but perhaps you have yet to concede — and correct me if I'm wrong — that many of those who have painstakingly arrived at another perspective are just as concerned about integrity and truth, personal and otherwise. Like you, I have no wish to believe lies, in which respect, as you suggest, we have much to learn from one another, given that neither of us has a monopoly on truth.

Switching gears, noteworthy news is that I might soon be shifting over your way. You'll recall that I applied for a job at Ormond College some months back. Apparently they passed on my details to Trinity next door, the Dean of which phoned me last week to ask if I'd be interested in a residential tutorship in English there, starting in February. I said yes, on the condition that we could come to a satisfactory financial and residential arrangement. Anyway, the Dean's away overseas and when he returns I'll no doubt be invited over for an interview. Of course, if I accept the position I'll need to supplement its meagre income with casual tutoring or teaching elsewhere, maybe through running an sf course for Melbourne Uni's equivalent of Adelaide's Continuing Education program. At this stage I find the whole idea appealing, since I feel I've gone about as far as I can in Adelaide and that perhaps it's time to explore fresh pastures. Plus I've always liked the idea of living in Melbourne. Besides, T has got the sf scene sewn up at Adelaide Uni, and the other two campuses aren't keen on the genre. Still, I aim to check out the Trinity offer carefully before making any final moves. I'm mainly concerned about the accommodation being up to scratch, that is, not too cramped or tastelessly modernised, and that the offer is financially viable.

Meanwhile, I'm disturbed to hear of your impending suffering of a tooth extraction. Gads, can't you get something done about it sooner? I don't like to think of you leaving it until the end of January, given that, as you'd know, infections can develop into more dangerous ailments. Not that it's any consolation, but as you might know, people who have trouble with wisdom teeth are supposed to be more highly evolved than those (like me) who don't, all to do with the evolutionary 'shrinking jaw' theory which supposedly gave us bigger brains and smaller mouths. Anyway, it will no doubt be a miserable time for you once the anaesthetic has worn off, so when the time comes, if you don't feel well enough to get done things you need to do, and if they're things I could do for you — shopping, cleaning, cooking, posting letters and the like — feel free to invite me to come over and help you out. I'm completely serious about this, so don't be too proud to ask. I assure you I have the time, inclination and health to make good the offer. And unlike you, I derive no macabre amusement from the suffering of my friends.

While we're in rebuke mode, you should know by now that you're not the only one who's a sucker for the intoxicating delights of the fantastic. I'm hardly pragmatic enough, save when friends need a helping hand, to qualify as an Isolde of the White Hand. While I don't mind cooking the odd roast chook, staying home to dutifully bake cup-cakes just ain't my style. I'd rather be imaginally soaring among the stars, and I welcome your company in doing so. Did you see the recent Hubble Telescope pics on the news? Images of protostars and nebular galaxies 12 billion lightyears away leave one dumbfounded. It's sort of eerie – in the right sort of way – seeing that far back in time, and sublime even to contemplate such staggering distances. As Jean-Luc Picard's deceased mum asked in a *TNG* episode: 'Do you see zis as zee end of za Universe, or perhaps as zee beginning of eet?'

Keep on boldly going where neither of us has ever gone before.

28 December 1994

Dear Damien

Sounds like you've been doing some gritty reading, what with Tipler, and Morrow's 'dead God' novel. I've just finished Dan Simmons' *Carrion Comfort*, a fat (992 p.) horror/sf novel about parapsychic violence – the ability of 'mind vampires' to control victims by altering brainwave frequencies. I haven't yet managed to get hold of the Thorne book on black holes, so when I come over for the Trinity job interview, perhaps you'd consider loaning it to me.

I did, though, recently enjoy Greg Benford's *Timescape,* specially the stuff in it about closed geometry universes within universes, and quantum tachyon time paradoxes. Interestingly, I had a tachyonic transmitter – my own idea at the time – in my early *Anddemar* draft. Did you manage to get your review of Penrose done? The only publisher I've heard back from lately is Oxford UP, who replied to my *Dreaming The Stars* proposal that they don't publish in this area. How unadventurous of them. Have you received any response from Melbourne UP to your proposed follow-up to *Arch of Babel* on 'fiction in the age of science'?

All that aside, while you have no hesitation in discussing your past, my reticence about my own is because it's for the most perceived as a blurred, detached web of memories containing nothing I wish to reiterate, obliterate, or otherwise dwell upon, nostalgically, tragically, or otherwise. And this is rather strange, given the overwhelming emotional avalanches I poured into so many of those now almost faded times. Perhaps it's because as an extremist, I seem to thrive on death-like transformations and cataclysmic reversals, which tend toward a ruthless severance of stale, outgrown habits, patterns, attitudes, and relationships.

You and I entertain divergent modes of perception and understanding, yet one need not preclude the other. We can discuss many things – love, life, archetypes, whatever – without needing, or being able to explain them (away). If we override, or at least take account of cultural dominants (namely, Western extraverted rationality vs Eastern introverted intuition), then our individual quirks are free to romp, and why shouldn't they, given that from a neutral perspective involving no à priori assumptions, reason is no more reliable than intuition and experience as a guide to truth, whatever 'truth' might mean. In the end, reason can neither undermine nor verify the certainty of gnosis.

Anyway, I'm sure that there are more things in heaven and on earth than are dreamed of in either of our philosophies. For Confucius, opposition was the prerequisite for union, since from within such creative tensions arises the urge to transcend them, a search which was symbolically amplified in Eastern and

Western alchemy. Opposing vantage points need not neutralise themselves into a stalemate, but can be — if we are humble and patient — transcended in a surprising 'Third' solution. I'm naturally drawn to such resolving syntheses, since rather than being neurotically indecisive I have a relativistic bent that comes from my quest for metaphysical fairness. Nonetheless, we tend to be more comfortable with what we value, condone, and are familiar with, which is why you've been such a surprise and challenge. You've reflected a side of myself, indeed an entire dimension of life that expresses the shadow which I've until recently ignored, or run away from.

Regardless of what we assume to be the norm, then, we begin with unprovable, often unstated assumptions of one sort or another. If appeals to the irrational at times support the kinds of 'ludicrous' claims you cite (demons and whatnot), reason has similarly justified just as many absurdities and atrocities; for instance, as Jung discusses, the Nazis' rationalisation of their quest for racial purity. I prefer the term 'transrational' as opposed to 'irrational', by the way, since the former denotes a synthesis of rational and irrational as that which transcends, rather than denies, reason.

As Bohr put it: 'Physics is not about how the world is, it is about what we can say about the world'. This relates to the 'myth' of objectivity, hence the deep division within the scientific community concerning the nature of reality, for instance, holists versus reductionists, both claiming adherence to uncompromising standards of scepticism and objectivity. Matter appearing out of and into nowhere, as well as events occurring without well-defined causes, don't yield readily to merely rational explanations. All theories, rational and transrational, are models and descriptions of how we perceive and interpret reality; they're not the reality itself, which is why scientific as well as non-scientific paradigms are always in a state of flux.

Quantum theory reminds us that the nature of reality will always depend in part on the questions we ask of it. In a similar vein and with more personal relevance, it's the theory which determines what we can observe. Who, then, is more scientific, the holist dominated, as Einstein was, by intuition, or the reductionist who privileges reason, given that the meaning of 'science' is from the Latin for 'knowledge'? Scientists, too, as individual persons have temperamental biases. But as for the reductionist/holist debate, perhaps when new questions take shape, both sides will ultimately be seen to be, at least some extent, ignorant. In the end, perhaps there's no ghost in the machine, because there's no ghost — and no machine.

Meanwhile I've been living out a well-known principle of physics, the 'law of natural indolence', or 'principle of least action'. The other night I stooped to watching that mind-blowing masterpiece, *The Giant Claw*, perhaps the worst and unintentionally hilarious sf movie of all time, though Ed Wood's *Plan 9 From Outer Space* is surely right up there with the 'best of the worst'.

1995 Letters

9 February 1995

Dear Suffering Tooth Loser

Good to hear that you're still in the land of the living. I almost fainted from nauseous *coinherence* – Charles Williams' term for sharing the suffering of others – whilst reading your vivid and grizzly account of your dental ordeal. Come to think of it, have you ever considered turning your writing talents to scripting horror movies? Remember that one about Joseph Mengele (played by Laurence Olivier) forcibly drilling holes in and extracting teeth from someone played by Dustin Hoffman? Anyway, I hope that after it was all over you resisted the morbid urge to retain the offending tooth fragments in a jar of formaldehyde, to be propped aloft somewhere as a grim reminder of the ordeal. What a strange thing is pain. As C. S. Lewis said, God whispers to us in our happiness but shouts to us in our suffering, or words to that effect.

Has your dentist replied yet to your amusing episodic letters? I'm sure they livened up his otherwise doubtlessly dull routine. Last year I loaned my dentist (at his request) my PhD thesis to read, but never received a response; it was merely returned in brown wrapping – like some porno novel – in the post. Still, I'm glad to hear you made good use of a packet of frozen peas during recovery mode. Which reminds me, I'm also glad you didn't attempt to return the cheese, yogurt and dips I left in your fridge, but thanks for boosting my dwindling tea-bag quota again. You probably also noticed that I didn't leave the chocolate at your place. I was a bit worried you might have wrecked even more teeth on it, so I selflessly ate it on the return flight home.

Reading Minds is a superb title for your 'new book' proposal. Will this be a sequel to *The Lotto Effect*? Your latest news from La Trobe sounds very encouraging, about time too. Hopefully you'll receive an offer of publication within a few weeks. A few days ago I got a note from B N declining my offer to review *Reading By Starlight* on the grounds that it was already scheduled to be reviewed elsewhere. Meanwhile, I still haven't found any takers for my Keats book. How dreary. I'm pleased to hear that *City Of Truth* made it through the post.

I savoured the extract you sent from your *Theory of Everything*, though my appreciation and comprehension of it was restricted by my ignorance of Jakobson's model. I'm not entirely clear what you mean by 'Code' as opposed to 'Text', for instance. Psychological and/or historically based theories of cyclic phases are intriguing; yours is, I feel, more credible, more intelligently considered and better researched than most, and you tie in the issue of ontogeny recapitulating phylogeny well. Your 12.5 year sections of 'Western lifetime' have a vague correspondence with Jungian individuation intervals, namely, the early awareness of a distinct ego ('social self'); 12.5–25 years as the isolation of the ego ('construction of ... individual self'); 25–37.5 as the reciprocal individuation phase (re-immersion in the objective/collective). As you imply, though, female phases would perhaps differ markedly in terms of distinguishing features. I wonder if Frazer's *The Golden Bough* could offer some relevant info concerning climatic and ecological cycles? You might be interested in the enclosed scrap about ancient Egypt, whose cycles seemed to depend on the lifespans of Pharaohs, and on climate changes.

You cite some convincing developmental and social analogues to your scheme, though I wonder how objective we can ever be about the length of cyclic intervals, given that this is determined by whatever distinguishing criteria we focus upon. And which is the causal factor, the psychological or the historical condition, that is, 'pulses in dominant temperament, controlled by physiological factors' versus other aspects as 'results of an underlying psychological change....' More bizarre, introverted theories, for instance, stress psychological causes and have included the Yeats/Blake/Plato vast *enantiodromian* cycles through which transexual 'male' and 'female' phases of consciousness alternate, as described in Yeats' 'A Vision'.

I was intrigued by your bracketing of Michelangelo and Byron, which may have a tenuous link with the bit of holistic lunacy I've enclosed — an extract from a talk I'm giving at the Jung Society next month. My basic 'theory' is that a spontaneous oscillation occurs between the 'I' (personal/subjective/introverted) phase and the 'We' phase (social/objective/extraverted), viz: Medieval-Classic 'We'/ Renaissance 'I'; Neoclassical 'We'/ Romanticism 'I'; Post-romantic 'We' as your empiricism/empire/ Modernism 'I'. Other weird ideas include the 2000 year cycles of astrological archetypes as a dominant paradigm of how the collective unconscious transforms the God-image, for example Aries: martial/egocentric 'I AM'/ Ram imagery; Pisces: dualism (God as 'good' vs 'evil' Devil)/altruism; Aquarius: holistic transcendence of all dualisms / divinity of humanity. Jung's writings on the *psychoid* (i.e. neither psychic nor objective) nature of UFO manifestations as a sign of this emergent holism are relevant here.

I see this major shift in our collective consciousness as the instigator of various new mythogenic trends in sf, from which, consciously or unconsciously, you, too, have not been immune. Thus to quote Zindell at the end of *Neverness*: 'Each of us ... we create this strange universe in which we live. We create God'. Or Maria, creator of the 'Autoverse' at the end of *Permutation City*: 'The whole idea of a creator tears itself apart. A universe with conscious beings either finds itself in the dust ... or it doesn't. It either makes sense of itself on its own terms, as a self-contained whole ... or not at all. There never can, and never will be,

Gods'. Of course, we can't postulate a causal scheme for such synchronistic cycles of evolution (if they exist); we must instead evoke a nonlocal mind/cosmos mirror relationship. I love your lapse into poetic mode with 'fractal foam' and 'combers of deep evolutionary tides'. Also, it's good to see you quoting Confucius. I look forward to reading the entire, hopefully soon to be published book.

I've been doing some silk painting, stencil designing and making-of-arty-things to sell at the upcoming 'Medieval Fair', a big annual event in the hills here. I never know in which direction my creativity will choose to flow next, given that it has a fairly even chance of going off on either a visual, musical, or verbal tangent. I'm even considering taking up the offer of a few musical gigs, self-accompanied on piano and acoustic guitar, at two well-known night spots, one very small, the other reasonably large, both medium-brow and dingily cosy.

We've just got things rolling again for this year's Mythopoeic Society meetings, with me in the Presidential chair. If you'd still like a spot as a guest speaker and are available for 21 April, we can cover your airfare.

Other news (tick one):

a. The Russian MIR space station and the US shuttle 'Discovery' have been visibly zipping across the skies at around 10 pm for the past few nights.
b. The original *Star Trek* series has just started screening here again on late night Channel 7.
c. A few days ago I watched a curious, innovatively produced show on SBS called 'The Art of Tripping', all about well-known, artistic drug users of the past century, including Aldous Huxley, who while on mescaline once 'saw the absolute in a fold of flannel trousers'. Next week they're moving on to PKD and Ballard.

d. I'm about to start on Greg Bear's *Queen Of Angels.*
e. All of the above.
f. None of the above.

To end on a winsome note, I hope we'll always care for and respect one another, no matter how this is expressed.

23 February 1995

Dear Damien

I hope it wasn't too melodramatic of me to phone you recently, but having not heard from you that week and knowing you'd been ill, I was getting very worried.

As I also mentioned on the phone, I've lost my Uni of SA teaching job because with all the slashing of funding going on, they've done away with the subject — and indeed the entire General Education program — and have replaced it this year with something unimaginatively called 'Broadening Undergraduate Education'. I've unsuccessfully tried to get my sf course onto this new prospectus, but they're too conservative to consider it seriously, so it looks like I'm stuck, for the time being at least, with running OCE courses, private tutoring, and giving 1 or 2 day workshops for the Jung Society. I've just applied for a lectureship in Children's Literature at the Uni of SA, which would be a neat job. If I got it I could probably smuggle some children's sf onto the reading list.

Moving on, thanks for your honesty in venting how you reacted to my visit. While there I was well aware of what you were feeling and the emotional strain of that rebounded to a large extent on me. I felt uncomfortable and apologetic and so tried to remain as unobtrusive as possible, not a hard task for me because I'm by nature a quietly independent person anyway. I enjoy the comfort of having someone else around, not just anyone though; it has to be a kindred spirit, someone who can potter about securely and contentedly centred in himself. In this respect my gut intuition toward you has been one of trust. I've never felt you to be a threat to my personal space, or my innermost being and ingrown soul. I have no less a desire and need than you have for personal space and freedom.

I hope you can appreciate, then, that it was painful for me not to feel welcome, given that the invitation to visit had come from *you* as something you seemed at the time to want. And so what I had looked forward to as at least a friendly visit turned into a deeply distressing time which, because I tightly controlled my feelings, I paid for dearly in terms of emotional pain — a partial ingredient of my recent 'illness' — after I'd returned home. I'm telling you this, I trust you understand, solely with the desire to be as open and honest with you as you have been with me. But I'm sorry as much as anything that we didn't at least manage to go for a walk, or out for dinner, or share an enjoyable adventure while I was there, especially after we'd done so much together while you were here.

On another level I felt privileged that you cared to solicit my response to your writing. My reaction to your work has always been emotional rather than intellectual, therefore not as articulate and helpful to you as I would like it to be. Certainly I was moved to tears with deep affection for the person who could write with such passion and enthusiasm for the kinds of concerns which fire my own soul, but which I cannot yet express with such sensitivity, insight and adroitness.

So I confess to being a little saddened by your recent, perhaps deliberate withdrawal from your letters of the simple fondness which friends usually have for one another. Perhaps you've done so with the mistaken belief that I might confuse such affection for something else. I assure you I never have, although I value this underrated *storge* variety of love as highly as any other expression of it. Indeed, if I had to choose between being your lover or your friend I would unreservedly choose the latter, although (in agreement with Johnson) I recognise that there need be no distinction between the two. And to whatever extent you care for me, I know you do so for who I am, not because I have embodied your longed for ideal. For this, as I've clarified before, I'm appreciative rather than disappointed. Dare I even say that what I've always felt from you, in spite of your lapses into defensiveness, anger, annoyance, or cynicism, is precisely love, not an idealised version of it, but more as a genuine, sometimes even gentle concern for my personal wellbeing, and again I'm touched by this.

I have no desire to invade anyone's life, least of all yours; nor have I ever allowed anyone to dishonour my own sacred space. I've only ever wanted to encourage and support you, while getting on with my own work, in whatever ways I can, even if it's only through sending cards and letters. Now I don't know whether I'd ever be welcome to stay with you again, given that I enjoy visiting Melbourne and would be content to sleep on the lounge for a few days' sojourn. You, of course, would always be welcome to stay with me, regardless of the relationship parameters.

So 'Yes' to a place with room enough for both privacy and company! Your idea of a shared spacious house with a spare bedroom sounds neither Victorian nor like an oddity to me, but would be, I agree, a necessity. I can certainly relate to it, since I'm absolutely useless unless I get a good night's sleep. Being a light sleeper, I'm easily blocked from obtaining it by loud snoring, psychic distress — my own and/or someone else's — or restlessness. It's not every day one meets someone who's happy to spend a lot of time listening to good music, quietly reading good literature, and intermittently discussing the insights and feelings these pleasant pursuits arouse. Such affinities of taste and temperament, in comparison with physical traits, become, I have found, increasingly valuable as life goes on, since they are the gifts which endure. This being the case, to feel close to you yet to be pushed so far away struck me as a tragic situation to be in.

Now that I'm back to the comparatively tranquil drawing board, it's a bit disorienting, though challenging and invigorating in a way, to have my energy fragmenting in all directions, partly in order to earn a crude buck. Still, there always seems to be some Strange Unifying Force causing all these tangents to overlap self-protectively. After all, we must take care, must we not, to imbricate our lives 'so that rain is shed without leaking inward to damage the vulnerable heart of things'. (Now who was it wrote that?)

I got a response from *Eidolon* to an Anddemaran short story I submitted in August 1993. The editors commented that 'despite the fact that the writing was good and the plot structure was strong and well-developed, there was a lack of development of and involvement with the characters, which reduced any dramatic impact the story might have had'. Oh well, it's useful to get some feedback anyway, no matter how late.

News flash: I just got a call from Uni of SA asking me to take a couple of two-hour classes per week on 'Language, Rhetoric and Reasoning', so I accepted. Imagine me encouraging the students into transcending reason by developing their intuition — what a rewarding challenge that could be.

On the music front, I've developed a penchant for Menuhin and Grappelli jazz playing, which I find delightfully uplifting to the soul. I've been re-appreciating Boccherini's well-known Minuet, which evokes an air of false dignity and playful, almost impish austerity. It always reminds me of that wonderful British black comedy *The Lady Killers*, in which a gang of bumbling criminals, masquerading as a string ensemble, plot their bank-robbing ploys in an old lady's rented upstairs room, to the tune of said Minuet. Delightful stuff and one of my Top 10 all-time favourite movies.

What great news about the US follow-up to *Lotto Effect*. Let's hope it's not just an idle promise and that something definite comes of it. I haven't read the Asimov biography and probably never will, since I'm not a big fan of his. The other day I found an intriguing passage in *Queen Of Angels*, a description of the 'Country of the Mind', which seems to blend together various perspectives on the nature of the collective unconscious:

> *It is a region, an unceasing and coherent dreamstate, built up from genetic engrams, preverbal impressions and all the contents of our lives. It is the alphabet and foundation on which we base all of our thinking and language, all our symbologies. Every thought, every personal action, is reflected in this region. All of our myths and religious symbols are based upon its common contents. All routines and subroutines, all personalities and talents and agents, all mental structures, are reflected in its features and occupants, or are reflections of them.*

It's ironic that while Jung's ideas are embedded in so much literature, literary journals on the whole snootily shun him. Dr David Tacey recently wrote to me:

> *Jung is Jung and literature is literature, and never the twain shall meet.... Take the journals first: literary journals are not at all interested, on the whole, mainly because Jung is not fashionable, and doesn't actually get a guernsey, not even in these days when 'literary theory' is so much to the fore. The Jung journals, on the other hand, don't have much time for literary exegesis — not unless it's racy, and always illustrates some larger archetypal concern, i.e. only if it subordinates the text to overriding psychological narratives.*

Did you know, by the way, that it takes at least seven photons to make the brain see light? And how come a light beam is 20 years long when space and time are interchangeable at the speed of light? I read this in your 1988 review of Richard Harland's *Superstructuralism,* which I haven't yet read.

Stay well, hopeful, and open to wonder.

17 March 1995

Dear Damien

Thanks for your letter, for the Davies book, and for your valued criticism of my *TNG* script. I've edited in some of your suggestions and enclose a patchy version of what I've done so far. As you rightly guessed, the opening 'emotional engagement' occurred on the missing page, in this case a romantic scene inspired by the crush I had on Jean-Luc Picard a few years back. Hence Xandde's personality is modelled entirely on yours truly, her hidden 'wild' side, that is. But the best scenes (so far) are the Ten Forward 'mindtravel instruction' one, and the one containing possibly the best joke in the history of *Trek,* where Data loses his head (literally) in a jousting tournament. [Worf drily asks him what he's learned from the ordeal, to which Data replies: 'Quit while you're a head'.] Anyway, the basic idea behind the script is that a primal quasi-consciousness — as a member of a species of energy which inhabits stars and from which our consciousness evolved — has been time-warped into the present, where it is seeking to understand what it will become. This is of course an inversion of Voyager's quest for its origin in the first *Trek* movie. The stellar being's blundering efforts are, predictably, interpreted as hostile by many and its questioned motivation causes conflict among the characters. I've written in other comments on the script and would of course appreciate any further suggestions you might be willing to add yourself.

When are your reviews of the Davies books scheduled to appear in print? Did you catch him and Frank Tipler discussing the search for ETI on ABC's 'Lateline' a few days back? Another noteworthy TV appearance on the same night was Stephen Hawking (obviously enjoying himself) on the holodeck, in the company of Data and sims of Newton and Einstein, in the *TNG* episode 'Descent' (Part 1).

The Disch book sounds like a worthwhile read. I've still got his *The M.D.* propped dustily on the shelf, waiting like so many others to be cued onto the 'must read' list. I've just finished a few oldies, including *The World of Null-A* which, aside from its fascinating denouement, I didn't enjoy as much as I expected I would. I've nearly finished Joan Vinge's *The Snow Queen* and enjoyed the settings more than I did the characters and plot. I've also read the Clarke/Gentry Lee novels *Cradle* and *Rama II*.

I confess that Clarke's style inevitably strikes me as pedestrian, untidy, unevenly textured, diversional, even juvenile (especially the dialogue) at times; plus his obligatory sexist stereotyping never fails to annoy, though it's not as overt as Heinlein's outright sleaziness. Why, then, am I always so keen to read Clarke's stuff? I think it's the guy's downright enthusiasm, optimism and sheer, almost childlike love of wonder and scientific plausibilities that never fail to delight and entertain.

In another recent read, Farmer's *Red Orc's Rage*, I was intrigued by the clinical afterword on 'Tiersian therapy', which one psychiatrist has used to treat psychotic disorders. As he writes concerning the 'World of Tiers' series: 'Its "Gates" provided the access mechanisms. Its characters were a Jungian delight; an entire panoply of archetypes were available for retrospective analysis. The variety of pocket universes presented a large but fixed number of multiple realities'. The novel also has a brief opening resonance with your *Sea*: 'How could he, seventeen years old ... know that he had created this seemingly ten-billion-year-old universe?'

Speaking of novels, your mention (in the context of Disch) of 'mental time travel to the middle ages' reminds me of Daphne du Maurier's riveting *The House on the Strand,* which haunted me for years with the desire to achieve what its protagonist did, minus his gruesome end.

Meanwhile, I'm mildly freaked out over job loss, attendant looming poverty and suchlike. Still, I'm enjoying teaching the 'Rhetoric and Reasoning' classes at Uni of SA, which will provide a financial buffer at least until July. The Arts students I'm teaching are, without exception, far more receptive, imaginative and intellectually curious than the predominantly Engineering and Computing mob I had last year. Plus the subject is more fun. I've even got them forming debating teams and writing plays to perform in class on matters such as euthanasia, woodchipping, and scientific innovations.

The other night my dear bro, the Fire Chief and Chef, took me to see the *Stargate* movie, which was far too 'gun-ho' American for my taste; but it had a sound core idea, namely the existence on opposite sides of the universe of parallel Egyptian civilisations, which in the past were connected by a space-gate that was dug up on Earth in the 1920s as an Egyptian artefact. Both civilisations were created by a lone alien in the guise of Ra, who gets about in a neat pyramid-shaped starship and is attended by Anubis and Horus-headed hench-aliens. Since one of the civilisations was forbidden to develop writing, they got stuck at the Egyptian era and the macho mob from Earth visit them through the stargate, then typically end up blasting poor old Ra to smithereens. As I recall, Phil Dick in one of his VALIS novels speculates that the Egyptians had been implanted with alien silver light-seeds, which accounted for their bizarre, seed-shaped head-gear and relatively enlightened status.

I'll write soon with similarly illuminating comments on your *Transreality* chapter.

Love and blessings

29 March 1995

Dear Damien

I haven't been completely honest about my book review of *Sea,* in part because my feelings for you have made it hard to maintain the detachment that's desirable for such ventures, for although, as you know, I can restrain an outward show of emotion, I neither can nor wish to deny to myself its reality. And yet I very much want to do the review, and whatever else I can to encourage you, and I find it frustrating to be hindered by that over which I have no control. Anyway, next week I'm driving down to the Inman Valley Youth Hostel for a few days and will take along the laptop with the aim of finishing said review.

Your *Transreality* chapter is wonderful, from its playful start readable, entertaining, insightful and ably supported by apt name droppings (better than mouse droppings, eh?), plus quoted passages. And as you say, it's about time this unique fictional mode was given its own term plus its fair share of the critical limelight. Certainly everything you write relates to the question of why life refuses to conform to our hopes and ideals. The truth of this always reminds me of T. S. Eliot's bit about the shadow falling between the 'idea' and the 'reality', a key theme in Modernist fiction in which the vindication of the iconic is superseded by the realism of psychological symmetry, namely the culturally suppressed shadow and light oppositions in Hardy, Conrad, Golding, Shaw, Forster, Lawrence, and others.

And as you make clear, PKD's characters are so weirdly unpredictable, therefore so believably human. If the Transrealist protagonist is 'neurotic and ineffectual', the cardboard Trek-like characters correspond to our inner ideals of ethical selfhood. Anyway, I look forward to reading the rest of your book, not least for its sheer exuberance and for the way your writing always inspires me to stumble on with my own efforts. I hope that your own inspiration continues to flow along the channels of least resistance, not only with this venture but with other literary pursuits. What you have to offer is always original, worth saying, and uniquely expressed.

On an altogether different note, something that continues to intrigue me is the psyche/cosmos connection inherent in the theory of a 'progressive, self-organising universe' as the mirror of the 'inherent ordering capability' of biological systems — and of the individuating psyche. Take, for instance, the structural transition in heated water from featureless 'cold' through the spontaneous emergence of order in 'warm', to the boiling disorganisation of chaos as a kind of chemical psychosis. A direct parallel exists in the ascription of the same adjectives to human emotional states, namely, the imbalanced negativity of coldness and hot-temperedness as opposed to the balanced personality as warm-heartedness.

In a similar vein we have the dimensionality of spacetime as a '3 + 1' quaternity, plus the four basic forces of Nature as mirrors of the four-fold structure of the psyche. In the collective psyche, the quaternity 'officially' emerged (as Jung predicted it would) in this century as the transformation of the God-image from one-sided, three-fold masculine to (3 + 1) four-fold, through the integration of the suppressed opposite — in this case the feminine — through the 1955 Catholic 'Doctrine of the Assumption' of Mary.

Dreary bits of news include the Uni of SA's withdrawal of the Children's Literature lecturer job, on the grounds that they didn't receive enough enrolments in the course. Routledge also let me know that they weren't interested in my Keats book, because they don't think they'd be able to sell enough copies of something so specialised. I've also applied for a lecturer job in English at Brisbane Uni. Kath Filmer, who runs the 'Fantasy and SF' course there, will likely put in a good word for me.

On a lighter front, this evening I'm off with our local ASTRA [Adelaide Star Trek Alliance] group to catch the new *Trek* film *Generations*. SASTREK, the biggest Trekker group in Adelaide, booked out the whole theatre for opening night and let us in on the act. From its playful start I found the movie engrossing, though it became somewhat predictable in terms of the obligatory goodies vs baddies outcome. It was a foregone conclusion that Kirk would end up joining forces with Picard and then sacrificing himself to save the day, thus ending his inordinately long life as the consummate hero.

Take care, Dayananda.

11 April 1995

Dear SATAC (Socialiser Among Toffs And Celebrities)

In view of your confessed 'evil' desecration of Rory's old novel, I thought that acronym-wise, 'Celebrities' would be preferable to 'Notables'.

I'm intrigued to hear of your ego-boosting, party-going escapades amidst the Bright Stars (well, White Dwarfs at least) of our nation. I'm also glad to hear that the 'biddie' you chatted to had the good taste to declare you a 'famous sci fi writer' rather than an almost famous one. Did someone shout you to a limo-lift for your homeward journey, or did you have to tram and train it back again?

Thanks for your comments on my *Trek* script. Yes, I suppose it was a useful exercise as much as a serious attempt, since I was aware when penning it that the series was winding up and that they weren't accepting further scripts. I enjoyed writing it, though, and had planned eventually to bring in Wesley and the Traveller to mind-zap the stellar energy being back into the past. Still, as you suggest, a novel might be a viable alternative, though I'd need a co-writer to handle the technical lingo and other plot hurdles. (Any offers?)

Meanwhile, I've decided to resurrect my old, autobiographical *Cross Connection* novel. My first task is to transcribe and edit the old typed text onto disk, which won't take long since it's a fairly short work anyway. At present it reads as a sort of metafictional, metaphysical, sf-ish piece of magic realism, which is fine if I can get it to work as such. Ideally, though, I'd like it to be more overtly sf-ish, but don't yet know how to go about it. Would you perhaps be willing to run your expert eye over any finished segments I might tentatively send over? I'm also attempting to revamp an sf story which a couple of years ago I sent to L R, who kindly (or politely, I suspect) remarked that he thought it 'lovely'.

I've enclosed a copy of a cat tale I just sent off. It's rather simple and unadventurous by your sophisticated standards, although this might add to its effectiveness as a vaguely sinister suburban myth. By a synchronistic coincidence, a nine year old moggie named 'Smoky' came to reside with me a few days ago. An acquaintance of mine, unable to find a new home for him, was going to get him put down, so I offered to take him in. We were getting along quite well, given that he clearly shared my bent toward indolent luxury. But now a cat-astrophe has occurred: the mog has disappeared! I've been reassured by a cat loving friend that, Dick Whittington-like, he's probably headed for his former home, so I hope this is the case, or at least that he's alright. Meanwhile, I've been leaving cat food outside in case he returns, and something, or somebody has been clandestinely nicking it. I'll see if I can catch the culprit in the act.

Other esoteric goings on: our next Mythopoeic meeting will feature my dear friend Dr Haydn Williams speaking on 'The Vanishing Hitch-hiker' and other eerie urban legends. Then in May we've got Colin Norris from UFO Oz International on UFO abductions, crop circles and whatnot, which I expect will draw a good crowd. We haven't yet lined up speakers for the rest of the year, in case you're still interested.

As well as wading through a pile of assessments for my Uni of SA classes, I'm putting together another round of talks for my next Uni of Adelaide sf course. I've put most of your books on the 'recommended reading' list, natch, including *R By S.* Next month I'm giving another talk at the Jung Society, this time on alchemy and the holism of Romantic imagination. They've also agreed to let me run an all-day workshop on 'sf and the evolution of myth'.

I'm pleased to hear that your inspiration is flowing into a revision of Rory's novel. It sounds like it'll be prudent for you to conflate this project with your ideas for your previously planned UFO book. The news on *Lotto Effect* also sounds encouraging. Wouldn't it be amusing, or at least ironic, if you ended up as some sort of parascientific guru, preferably with the Templeton Prize in tow?

I just got another dismal knock-back, this time from Uni of WA Press, who said that my *Dreaming the Stars* proposal wouldn't 'fall within [their] established list'. And speaking of (your speaking of) 'ethno-specific viruses', I've just finished Orson Scott Card's *Xenocide.* I've also just enjoyed Asimov and Silverberg's *Nightfall,* since I love tales set on worlds with multiple suns, though my favourite will always be David Lindsay's work of mystical genius, *A Voyage to Arcturus.*

I like your answering machine message. By 'genius' do you mean the original connotation of the word as one's 'guiding spirit'? The latter could be inferred from the somewhat ambiguous wording of your message, in other words the suggestion that for some reason said spirit has peevishly run away from home.

Please send over more of your *Transreality.* And what was wrong with Rory naming a psychotic character Damien?

Love and blessings

4 May 1995

Dear Extremely Productive And Entertaining Writer

As always, it was good to hear from you. Did my tiger eye whizzo silver letter opener reach you in time for your birthday? I sent it on the same day I posted the card.

It grieves me a little that I upset you by calling you a 'Funny Old Thing'. Goodness Damien, do you dislike yourself so much that you can't accept even a simple gesture of fondness? I assure you it was purely an affectionate whim on my part. It had nothing to do with your age — I often call my 7 year-old godson a 'Funny Old Thing' — nor did it allude to your recent hobnobbing with luminaries. I was in fact happy to hear that you were getting out and about socially, knowing as I do your proneness to sitting in front of books propped open by rubber bands for hours on end, while your neck is killing you.

Surely you know that I'd never wilfully do or say anything either to hurt or humiliate you. I respect you too much to call you an 'Old Fart' and if you managed to retrieve my last letter from your inundated desk, you'll see that I was implying you were the opposite of this. Besides, as I recall 'Funny Old Thing' referred (in the context of my letter) to your amusing answering machine message. Details aside, I have no desire or ability to relate to you on a purely cerebral level, even in letters. I'm not primarily a cerebral woman, neither, thank the gods, are you a merely cerebral man.

Anyway, it sounds like you had a fruitful birthday in the form of producing an 11,500 word story. Heck, this is impressive, given that I feel I'm being prolific if I manage to churn out 1000 words a day. I'm pleased to hear that your lava-like creative energies are flowing fiercely, or rather gushing forth like a preceding volcanic eruption. Your description of current literary irons in the fire (excuse the pun) makes wonderful news, and I'm particularly relieved to hear that you intend to return to *The White Abacus,* given that your original ideas for it sounded, to say the least, brilliant. 'Keeping yourself busy' indeed. Don't ever let the fire go out, Dayananda. The world needs your extraordinary talent. Speaking of talents, I'm always both challenged and consoled by Christ's injunction to 'do the best you can with what you've got', or words to that effect. Hence I plod along with my *Cross Connection* novel, content that I'm at least writing.

I hope your Dog story gets accepted by *Omni.* What's happening with the radio version, or have I missed it? It seems that somewhere along the line I've definitely missed your reviews of the last two Paul Davies books. What an amazing soul you are to be able to juggle all these demanding projects. It inspires me to get on with my own stuff, I can tell you. What a nifty idea to do a sequel to *Dreaming Dragons.* I still think a film version of it, perhaps directed by Peter Weir, could work well.

Glad to hear you're keeping the post-grads in line. On the subject of cyberspace, I was recently riveted by Bruce Sterling's non-fictional account of hackerism, *The Hacker Crackdown.* It's fascinating how the whole digital underground is becoming a new kind of questing environment in which heroes and anti-heroes jostle and esoteric overtones abound; for instance, forbidden knowledge being the basic currency, plus many suffering an obsession to teach and spread the hacking ethos.

Outlaws, cults, rebels, pioneers, all with imaginative, mythic pseudonyms – Knight Lightning, Knights of Shadow, Legion of Doom, Neon Knights, Prophet and Shadowhawk – seem to interface myth with cyberpunk scenarios. The psychological ramifications are intriguing when we view the entire networking environment as a wholism whose dark and light facets are underscored by the moral neutrality of information technology. The whole thing operates like a living organism. I 'saw' the other day how it even simulates the consequences of gene replication error, as occurred in the 1991 July 1 US Crash, when one tiny typographical flaw in one single line of the software, for which 7 million lines of code are usually needed, deprived the whole nation of its phone service. Sterling also gives fascinating accounts of his brushes with the law when he collaborated with well-known hackers to write his cyberpunk novels. I recently read his *Islands in the Net* but didn't enjoy it as much as I thought I would, since it was too much in the spy thriller vein for my taste.

At present I'm writing a lengthy treatise to Whitley Strieber, detailing my own numerous numinous experiences, several of which – including my countless dreams of being hunted by UFOs – resonate with his own alien encounters. Reviewing his *Transformation*, I've been struck by his recurrent use of individuation symbols as well as metaphors for explorations of the collective unconscious. Significantly, the nature of his encounters with 'the Visitors' affirms my own understanding that the shift into holism involves a new phase of consciousness in which dualism is superseded by unity on all levels of awareness and existence. Strieber seems to share this intuition, as is apparent in his reflections on the mode of perception through which these meetings occur. He comments on the merging of objective and subjective, inner and outer, which validate Jung's designation of the collective unconscious as the 'objective psyche', the unifying matrix of archetypes as the psychoid forms of godlike forces. Hence Strieber notes 'the subjective nature of the experience, and how it appears to flow from an objective reality, but is changed by the filter of our perceptions', while the aliens are described as 'an objective reality that is almost always perceived in a highly subjective manner'.

All this is of course the essence of synchronistic phenomena as eruptions of archetypes into the phenomenal realm. Predictably, then, Strieber's aliens reflect the evolution of consciousness, that is, Jung's proposal that ruling dominants age, thereby bringing about what he called a 'metamorphosis of the gods', such that (in Strieber's words) 'we know that their appearance depends more on the understanding of reality through which a given culture perceives them than on any objective insight into their true nature. With this in mind, it seems to me almost inevitable that we would, at this point in our technological and cultural development, see them as space-faring aliens'. Allied comments include: 'I thought of the gods of old, all the visitations and apparitions that have, taken together, formed almost the whole of our religious experience. They have taught us everything we believe, in virtually every religious tradition'.

A key correlation with holistic philosophy and psychology includes the mirroring of microcosm and macrocosm, whereby the 'unconscious mind is like the universe out beyond the quasars. It's a place we want to go to find out what's there'. Then in the chapter titled 'A Soul's Journey' he sees 'a large object that seemed to be made of clay. It was round on one side and square on the other, and was rotating slowly. The square and round parts separated and began circling one another.... It seemed to represent a reconciliation of opposite forces, a sort of "squaring the circle"'.

This latter example of the Philosophers' Stone relates to the Dream I had last year of you and me having our minds imprinted with cosmic techno-mandalas, by twin alien craft which orbited each other like a binary star. Both visions, in other words, share the same psychological significance in being symbolic dramatisations of the union and dynamic tension of opposites. Strieber also has various dreams of fields of flowers, which similarly occurred in my Dream of you and me, when someone crossed a field of flowers and handed me a bunch of them over a fence.

Strieber's associated phenomena include various symbolic confrontations with the shadow. As well, his recurrent and frightening journeying into the woods can be viewed as a metaphoric confrontation with the collective unconscious. Equally significant is the moral ambiguity of the aliens and Strieber's emotional ambivalence – inscribed by the poles of fear and love – toward them. Notably in this respect the Visitors' primary method of communication is symbolic, or theatrical. Strieber's dream of a huge eye (as God/self/soul) looking down on him in the woods brings to mind PKD's 'Eye in the Sky' visions. One could go an *ad infinitum* but a few other parallels with my own dreams and visions are worth mentioning.

Firstly, a couple of scary apocalyptic dreams: Strieber had one in which a vast nuclear plant exploded when masses of pipes that lined its walls erupted with water and sent people screaming off in all directions. I had an almost identical dream, except that the pipes were underground and shot steam into the air before the plant blew up. (Water is of course a symbol of unconscious forces.) Strieber also dreamed of the moon exploding and of the resulting fragments destroying the Earth. In a terrifying dream I had, the sun was darkened and in Ptolemaic fashion fell out of the sky toward the Earth, as people scurried about trying in vain to brace themselves for the impact. (The darkening of the sun symbolises the fading of a conscious dominant, an exploding moon the destructive power of unconscious forces.) Strieber also discusses 'Keltic Factor Red', a so-called 'star language' which people who have had encounters speak under hypnosis and which is strongly Celtic in content. This fascinates me in view of my own Welsh heritage and because almost all the names that spontaneously 'came' to me for my Anddemaran mythology sound Celtic. Some, as I later found out, even mean what they symbolise; for instance 'Selwynd', which means 'White Rider' and is the name of one such being in an orbiting galaxy. Strieber's dreams and visions of wolves and owls also echo dreams I've had.

As a postscript, a few nights ago I dreamed I was in a large, two-storied house, in a room of which a vast collection of exotically coloured, mysterious rocks was displayed on shelves. I picked up one of these rocks and immediately began to levitate off the floor. When I got near the high ceiling I automatically inverted and landed feet first on this upside-down floor. Annoyingly, though, the dream was interrupted at this point by the phone ringing very early in the morning.

Coming back down to Earth, thanks for your comments on my cat tale. As a bizarre epilogue to my (non-Cheshire) Vanishing Cat saga, the lady a couple of houses away just acquired a grey male cat (as mine was) named 'Smoky' (as mine was.) Could there be some kind of odd synchronistic karma at work here? I did, however, finally catch the stealthy critter which was whiska-ing away the cat food I'd been leaving outside. It was an old Siamese belonging to an old guy down the road. Alas, no more felonious freebies for this feline, I fear.

Good to hear that *The Stars My Destination* is scheduled to be made into a movie, as is revealed in Galaxy Bookshop's latest *Nexus*. I see that you also get a mention in the 'Grapevine' column where they note that you've been granted another Writing Fellowship, 'apparently' to write your 'ninth sf novel'. Interesting as well that you should mention P F; I'd in fact phoned him on the day I received your last letter to ask if he'd like to sell books at our Mythopoeic gatherings. He said he would. I've also been liaising with J G, who's kindly offered to give a talk on sf at our June meeting. This should prove to be a useful follow-up to Colin Norris's UFO talk coming up in a few weeks' time.

I've just cooked up a nice Mongolian roast of lamb. Wish you were here to share it with me!

Seeya round the galaxy (as the cetologist in *The Voyage Home* said to Captain Kirk).

Thought for the day: 'We're one possible solution to a giant cosmic anagram'. (Greg Egan)

12 May 1995

Dear Damien

I've just tottered over to R's in the PhilDickmobile – the door of which is still jammed shut – to pick up *The Book of Revelation* and have at his invitation a cup of tea and a chat. Your manuscript should provide an effective counterbalance to the dull pile of marking I'm wading through for my Uni of SA classes, so I look forward to having a good read this week. I've also just finished *Against A Dark Background* by (as you'd know) the brilliant and sometimes very funny Iain Banks. The guy certainly produces some vividly memorable scenarios, for instance the one in which a band of privateers called 'Solipsists' attack a city:

> *Their attack on the fringe of the Log-Jam had not been an unqualified success. They had heard there was a convention of circus performers taking place on a hotel-ship ... and so disguised themselves as a troop of three-legged mutants, with their guns inside their hollow legs.... But they'd got their dates wrong; the convention wasn't for another month.*

After chuckling over this I proceeded to swoon over his marvellous names for planets and moons: Thrial, Trontsephori,

Speyr, Roaval, Plesk, Vio, Prenstaleraf, Phrastesis, all Scottishy names that demand to be savoured and spoken aloud.

Thanks for your sound advice about Whitley Strieber. If the guy's mad he's mad — and probably therefore am I. If, as you suggest, he's a notorious liar that's of course another matter that leads me to having second thoughts about sharing my own experiences with him. Fortunately I hadn't yet posted anything off. It seems to me that he relies a helluva lot on plagiarising Jung's insight, which was always based on his observation and experience, concerning the anatomy and dynamics of the psyche. I must admit I had my doubts about the authenticity of certain claims Strieber made, for instance his statement that his 7-year-old son actually said aloud that the 'unconscious mind is like the universe out beyond the quasars. It's a place we want to go to find out what's there'. Hmm. A bit too shrewd and eloquent for one so young, methinks, and judging by my 7-year-old godson's level of articulation.

Still, if Strieber has lifted his material not only from Jung but also from other occult literature — which would certainly account for its archetypal overtones — it still begs the question of where such material came from in the first place. I, for one, don't need to believe in the truthfulness of Strieber's claims when I've had similar visions and dreams myself, as have others such as Blake, Jung, and Phil Dick. I certainly have no reason to doubt the integrity of such wise, shrewd, honest, humorous and benevolent souls, none of whom, I'd say, would have been in it for the money. But of course the actual nature of such experiences, the question of whether they originate from some other primary mode of reality, will always be open to debate. What can't be doubted by those who've experienced such things is the unnerving and sometimes disorienting reality of the experiences themselves. Meanwhile, though, I'll look out for Schnabel's *Dark White*.

Thanks for sending me the extract from your *Book of Revelation*. Needless to say it left me wanting to read more. I liked your landscape and spacescape descriptions and the restrained use of short bits of dialogue. The whole passage builds up with laid-back suspense to its denouement, though of course I knew in advance what the 'revelation' would be. Concerning your *Transrealness*, I'm surprised to hear of the surly response from S; I'd have thought he'd have been pleased to hear you were promoting the transrealism cause, so it strikes me as petty of him to quibble over your use of 'transreality'. Perhaps you need to strike him off of your Christmas list. I hope Melbourne UP have finally contracted you for the book, regardless of his grouchy remarks.

I'm glad to hear the C family invited you over for a birthday dinner. I've been juggling a few social engagements, including visiting friends and rellies with my other brother, the younger one who works as a fire officer at the Woomera Space Station. I've also been spending quite a bit of time helping out my 'single mum' pal, who phoned me while I was staying with you, and who's been hobbling about on crutches after tripping over during a recent trip to New Zealand. My folks are also off to NZ next week for another holiday, so I'll most likely camp at their place for a few weeks and do some more writing, tinkling on the piano, and preparing more talks for my sf course and my upcoming Jung Society lecture.

On to inevitable personal matters: re the obviously worrying concerns you raised in your last letter, there's not much I can say, given that we've covered a lot of this ground before, except to state the (to me) obvious, namely that ultimately it's mutual kindness and acceptance more than shared beliefs that hold any worthwhile relationship together. I've always felt and done my best to express such an attitude to you, which is why I've no wish to argue over which of us is more guilty of taking the other too seriously, or missing the point of jokes, or whatever. So we both have our faults, weaknesses and blind spots; we're human, after all, and such flaws are part of the package. Why not focus instead on the good and commendable qualities we see in one another, which I've always seen in you — and which you seemed more ready to see in me when we first began communicating? One example was your generous response to my old Christian music, your readiness to appreciate its likeable aspects. When we were first writing to each other you seemed delighted, even eager to receive and reply to my letters, which in turn led to your wanting us to spend time together, thereafter to your reflection that this time had been (at least) pleasant for you. Why then can't we return, or rather move on to focusing on what we like about one another, or is this no longer a viable option for you?

Maybe I'm asking too much, for it seems that me affectionately calling you a Funny Old Thing has (rather absurdly) opened, or rather reopened the proverbial can of worms regarding the desirability, or otherwise of our different takes on reality. While I take your point about us each at times misreading the other's intentions, meanings, or verbal playfulness, I don't attach the importance that you do to such glitches, given that they seem, to me at least, to be comparatively minor slip-ups when pitted against what is successfully shared by us both. But of course that's only how I see it.

We're always open to being misinterpreted in writing letters, as in all other forms of communication, though I'd say we've both done a good job of tackling the blind spots once they've arisen. And you're right, of course; I fail to see what the fuss is about our delightful differences. I know you don't see it in this positive light, but haven't we gone over this ground before? I might add that it does puzzle me, though, why you continue to be so irritated, disturbed, even threatened by my and others' spiritual approach to life, when I'm at ease with the equal validity of your own world view, which is one reason why I've always admired and enjoyed your writing.

We see and relate to reality differently. So what? Isn't that the whole point of it taking all kinds to make the world? And if our shared delight in the fantastic means as much to you as it does to me, isn't this overlap of loves at least as important as our differences? Last year you wrote that you believed we had 'much to learn from one another'. Do you no longer see this as the case? If to you our differences outweigh our overlapping interests, how can my friendship continue to have any overriding value for you? It comes down to this, surely, that as long as you continue to view our differences in a negative light you will continue to promote discord between us. And as long as I see it otherwise I shall encourage and seek harmony. Certainly I'd never push you away, or reject you, or withdraw my offer of support and friendship. These moves can only ever come from you.

What you see negatively as 'dissonance' I've always viewed as creative tension, but perhaps our contrary perspectives will never change; I don't know. Of course I accept, then, that relationships can thrive on the challenge of the Complementary Other, but only when there is mutual respect and affection. After all, if our ideological differences are the whale-sized bones of contention you make them out to be — and I don't subscribe to your overestimation of their size — we could hardly share the mutual respect we apparently have for one another. How, for instance, could you be willing for me to write a book about you if you didn't in some sense welcome the legitimacy of my perspective? And even if I don't fully relate to your stance on life, I can appreciate the unique view it offers, because that's essential to who you are and I'd never wish you to be otherwise.

So what are you saying underneath what you're saying in your last letter? That you'd like me to be different? Do you wish I was more like you, or more like other women you've known? Would you rather I tried to conform to your ideals, or that I agreed with every word you said? If you can only care for, or befriend, or even merely like someone who is predominantly like you, or conforms to your ideal feminine side, isn't that just another sublimated way of seeking self-love and approval? I'm led to wonder what exactly you've expected from me. Did you expect analytical pragmatism? Or a lack of interest in matters esoteric? I don't know what your current attitude is, but isn't Wolff's 'medium' phase the very type you suspected might be your fourth and final phase of relatedness to women? Has it ever occurred to you that Wolff's Jungian '3+1' quaternity cautions that the fourth will differ radically from the other three, since it (she) represents the difficult challenge of the unintegrated opposite who embodies your shadow, just as you embody mine?

I love you, but I'd never change myself for you, even though I recognise there's room for improvement on certain fronts, which is why I've been getting up early most days to do an hour's Callanetics. But all in all I like myself the way I am, even though in recent months — after being pushed away by you when I stayed with you in January — I've had to struggle to regain my self-esteem, but have now done so, partly through my own uncanny ability to reboot myself, but equally through the warm companionship of friends and family. To be precise, late last year your unfavourable comparison of me, however indirect, with other women you've been involved with hurt me deeply, as you must surely have suspected it would. But after quietly working through this I decided that if you were happy for us to remain friends, I'd be glad for us to be so.

The wound was reopened when I visited you in January. If, as you formerly confessed, you had forebodings about my visit, or had intended to distance me physically and emotionally, why, I still wonder, didn't you simply put me up on the lounge? Still, I've been gradually healed of these memories now and know that you could never hurt me in this way again, even if you didn't at the time intend to cause such pain. All I can add, then, is that my wish has only ever been to reach out to you, emotionally, intellectually and physically, in companionship and affection. But I've continued to relate to you on the level *you've* chosen because I'm always challenged, or inspired, or delightfully entertained by what you share, and because I remain concerned about your personal well-being.

My affectionate gestures have thus been merely one way of saying, or rather not saying, that I care for you. 'Funny Old Thing', for instance, was not meant to be taken in a semiotic or hermeneutic context, nor as a gag. As I've said, I have no desire to relate to you on a purely cerebral level, and you've expressed enough sensitivity and emotion in your own fiction and letters to know how vital feelings – whether helpful or harmful – are to human relationships. As well, even though you downplay it in your last letter, your self-love, or lack thereof, still seems to be a thorny issue with you. It certainly surfaces in your cynical response to my confessed respect for you, given that such respect doesn't imply that I see you as 'awesome and godlike'. Respecting you means recognising and appreciating your integrity and worth, qualities which you seem unable or unwilling to perceive in yourself.

I know that what I've said so far will probably anger you, but I'm willing to take that risk if it's what you need to hear. I merely suggest that it might throw some light on our situation. Perhaps it all comes down to the simple truism that if you don't love yourself then it's hard to love, or accept love from others. And let's face it, deep down, no matter how much you hide behind your scathing exterior, like the rest of us you need to love and be loved. But if you won't let go of your past relational hurts, disappointments and ideals, how will you ever grow beyond your narrow expectations, or be reconciled to your inner wounds, or welcome whatever gifts life may be offering you? I can ask this because these are lessons I've had to learn and at least to some extent have learned; as I've made clear before, you were a far cry from my ideal man.

I realise this probably all sounds simplistic, but then truth is often simple. After all, what do all your brilliant achievements amount to if you don't love yourself and if you don't have someone to love you? I suppose I'm simply saying that such love, even if it is the Isolde of the White Hand variety, will remain here for you, should you ever choose to accept it. And if you don't, well, I'll say this much on my behalf: you'll never find a more loyal, devoted and supportive friend. I'll add this about you. In your good self I've finally met my match and I regret nothing that's happened, or that's been said, or written between us. Thanks again, then, for allowing me to be part of your life and for teaching me so much about what it means to be human — and sometimes painfully alive.

Gads, did I say there wasn't much I could say on the concerns you raised? As far as I'm aware, I haven't taken your last letter amiss, so I hope to get a similar response from you. For my part I'm merely trying to inject more honesty into our relationship, since some of what I've shared I've until now — perhaps unwisely — kept to myself. To tell the truth, though, I'd much rather we were jointly exploring the likes and loves which inspire us to reach for the stars.

Bless you, Dayananda.

31 May 1995

Dear Brooding Wanderer Of Streets And Rooms

Thanks for your long epistle. To be honest, I'd begun to suspect that you were beginning to dislike me, and since if that were true there's little I could do about it, I was questioning the worthwhileness of continuing our communication. So even if it sounds a trifle neurotic, there were things you said which I needed to hear, or needed to be reassured of, and you're wise enough to know what they were. Anyway, I appreciate your saying what you did with such artful tact and openness. As for me, I've chosen to tell you the truth (as I see it) regardless of the personal cost to myself, and I find it hard to believe that deep down you'd wish me to do otherwise. I've always trusted my intuition in writing to you, even — or rather especially — when it's gone against the counsel of my mind. Or in old-fashioned terms I could say that my heart always rules my head.

I've always suspected that your anger is to some extent reactionary to your hated Catholic background, and who can blame you for rejecting any form of dogmatic, puritanical fearmongering? But of course, as with all reactionary psychological moves, the un(hog)washing often means throwing out the baby with the bathwater, or in this case the God with the holy water. It's we humans, after all, who have turned Christ's original message of love into an overemphasis on hellfire and damnation. In the ousted Gnostic Gospels, 'sin', for instance, is ignorance rather than naughty actions that warrant divine punishment. Even Jung had a vision of God dropping a huge turd on a church — perhaps God's way of announcing that all our theologising has got it wrong, or at least made God one-sidedly heavenly.

Of course I want to keep communicating with you, even though I'll go on missing you and wanting to be with you as well. Although I've had many good friends and several not so good lovers (excluding you), for most of my life I've been deprived of the quality of communication we share, and now that I've found it I've come to treasure it and hope not to lose it. Let's face it, in terms of integrity, intelligence and a commendably playful seriousness about life, friends of your calibre are hard to come by. I'm well aware that what I say sometimes annoys or angers you. But to turn the tables, if you can accept that I'm no masochist, have you ever wondered why I persist in writing to you when I'm the dill on the receiving end of your outbursts?

Don't worry, I can take your eruptions of anger or annoyance, firstly because I know that they're a necessary venting of what you're dealing with inside, and secondly because I've always sensed that deep down no personal malice toward me has ever been intended. Besides, there's a healthy lack of repression about it that I find quite wholesome, though of course — as I'm glad you realise — those who mean well toward you can get bruised in the process. But as you confess, it's your problem and commendably you're not running away from facing it.

I was, if you'll forgive me, bluffing when I claimed to be 'puzzled' by your hostility to holists. I hope this doesn't sound too amateurishly psychotherapeutic, but then the amateur is by definition moved by love. My instinct is always to heal, and I suppose I can't help being enthused when I sense that someone I care about is beginning to explore their infinite inner potential. (Of course you've always been aware of the boundless wonder of the universe 'out there'.)

As a holist, Jung never separates the greater Unity from the human psyche, which is his point of contact with quantum holists and Eastern mysticism. The central mystery here is the mirror relationship between psyche and Nature, which is an intuitive insight that defies analysis. Conscious reason can't unite the opposites; irrational intuition, by drawing on the unconscious, can. To my way of seeing it, the blockage which most thinking extraverts face with understanding 'holism' is that they evaluate it solely on their own terms, which are presumed to be more reliable criteria of truth. Namely, they assume holism to be a rationally proposed, external consensus reality, and (as a corollary) they employ the inappropriate yardstick of reason to evaluate its validity.

Intuitive introverts find all this horribly unfair, of course, and resent having to produce tedious apologetics and factual evidence for what they know through bypassing logic. To add insult to injury, they are forced to pander to the rational bias of empirically minded 'thinking types' in the bargain. You can't prove that reason is superior to intuition. The best you can do is to start with the untestable assumption that it is. Attempts to disprove the validity of intuition can only be done through circular reasoning that presumes the superior reliability of a rational stance. My point has been that, psychologically speaking, both are equally valid preferences – and equally subjective ones.

While I don't doubt that we're both open-minded, sincere and inquisitive, because of our distinctive backgrounds and temperamental predispositions neither of us is completely unbiased. Have you noticed, for instance, that you evaluate credibility solely in terms of rational and objective criteria? Again, I'm not being judgmental here, merely trying to throw more light on (what you call) the 'dissonance' between us, so I'm not for a moment suggesting that your perspective is wrong, merely that it's one slant of a whole picture that needs both of our angles, just as we need male and female, dark and light, east and west, fish and chips, rock and roll, whatever.

In Jungian terms, by being prickly toward my mystical and holistic bent, you're projecting your shadow, as we all do to some extent. Here the infallible guideline is that the more we become aware of doing it, the less power it has over us; that is, we then have some say in the matter. Perhaps deep down, as I've always felt to be true, you're really battling yourself rather than other people. In fact your term 'the not-self foe' is an exact paraphrase of the *alter ego* as the rejected side of oneself, and nothing is more important in individuation than befriending this disliked, repressed, or feared shadow. When we stop running away from it and turn to face it, it often turns from being a foe into becoming an ally in our instinctual drive toward wholeness.

For Jung, God (as an archetype) is at the very least the centre and circumferential whole of the unconscious, but then what is the unconscious? How little we know about it. It certainly doesn't experience time and space the way consciousness does, so in one sense it's another genre of reality. This is where Jung achieves the miraculous, ironically enough by saving 'God' as an archetypal human experience from the sorry fate of obsolescence *as a religious belief*. Similarly, mysticism isn't about injecting God, or Mind, or whatever into the machine (an extraverted, dualistic metaphor anyway); it's about the inner experience of numinous and transrational eruptions from the unconscious as the origin of all religious phenomena. As I see it, the approach to knowledge you allude to isn't primarily about differing beliefs, but is rather a matter of temperamental bias. And that's neither right nor wrong; it's simply an unavoidable and perhaps desirable quality of human existence.

The reason why the boundaries between science and religion are being eroded is that both are firmly grounded in the subjectivity of the human psyche. Hence the more that quantum theorists have taken into account the subjective state of the observer, the more comfortably they've aligned themselves with a holistic stance. Again, to the introvert this trend is more intriguing as psychological truth than as historic fact.

Two key paradoxes of holistic philosophy throughout the ages have always been the mirror relationship between microcosm and macrocosm, and the experiential and symbolic coincidence of God and self as the central reality of the psyche. The key word here is 'reality', since to the introvert — as Jung always stressed — the inner life of the psyche is as real as outer facts. Throughout my own life I've certainly known this to be true. Still, if you think I'm an extreme introvert now you should have seen me ten years ago when I was unwillingly and fearfully confronting, head-on and alone, the awesome power of the (masculine) animus archetype. At the time I was treading a perilous tightrope between sanity and madness and almost went under; that is, I was nearly swamped by the power of the unconscious. Indeed, if the worst had happened I'd most likely now still be at the funny farm muttering prophecies about God and/or the Devil to the guys in white.

As a consequence, I've had to learn to welcome the outer reality of often harsh facts. I tentatively suggest, then, that you have yet to confront the equally demanding inner reality of your unconscious, for it's only here that you'll ever again face the God-image, this time as your true self — and we can't reject one without denying the other. Of course none of us ever gets to the end of this sometimes dark and isolating road, but until we make a start we can never be reconciled to 'the God within' and to the marriage of opposites which this union midwifes.

In contrast, the problem with a lot of overly optimistic New Age thinking is that it loses touch with the perennial philosophy's flow of intuition and stagnates by congealing into dogma (about crystals, spiritual development, or whatever), opinions, and borrowed beliefs, precisely what the Church did by losing touch with the subterranean stream of archetypes to which it owed its rise. All this happens because New Ageism is dominated by (what Jung calls) the 'feeling function', which is very strong on relationships, vibes and values, but weakest when it comes to critical thinking.

In comparison, Catholicism is far more intuitive than rational. Unlike you having to endure Catholic dogma and hellfire threats at a young age, about ten years ago I was drawn to the Catholic Church precisely by its inclusion of the irrational, by its symbolic and mythic backdrop, and by its integration (however distorted) of the feminine principle so ruthlessly shunned by Protestant logic. My leaving it arose from a recognition of the pitiful inadequacy of both its patriarchal, legalistic God-image and its infantile model of the Cosmos. Plus Christ appeared to me in a vision and beckoned for me to follow Him out of a Church window and along a beam of light, thence into vaster pastures that included all religions as expressions of the life of the psyche.

Thankfully, no form of religion was ever foisted on me as a child. Instead we had a *soulful* upbringing, immersed in music, art, books, gardens, outdoor play, and the occasional steam train ride. My grandfather worked on one such train, which drove past his home at regular times. Whenever I stayed with my grandmother, we'd stand outside and wave to 'Granfer' as the train, blowing its whistle, puffed and chugged past. The quest for 'truth' is one I embarked on passionately at an early age. I can still recall the moment. I was 8 years old, lying on the grass and staring up at the sky one sunny day, when I pledged myself to this very quest. Unfortunately, though perhaps it was fatefully necessary, after an intensely spiritual experience of being rescued by Christ from a paralysing attack by evil forces and then 'reborn' in the Spirit, I got bogged down in various Protestant scenes that were way too rational, and too lacking in a sense of mystery for my taste.

Eventually I encountered Jung, whose writings made sense of a subsequent acute spiritual crisis, namely a gradual, destabilising and profound shift of the gravitational centre of my consciousness from the 'peripheral' ego to the paradoxical, core self. Handing over the reins of my life to this new inner authority transcended conscious knowledge, because it embraced the wisdom and guidance of the unconscious. One can only deny, or suppress the reality of the unconscious by clinging to the one-sidedness of the ego. Sooner or later though — and this applies to all of us — it's gonna getchya. My arrival in the Jungian camp, in summary, was simply the next stop along the way (Tao) of my personal trek.

I'm all too aware that in other areas of experience and understanding you're lightyears ahead of me. Somehow you manage to fine tune life's bizarre blend of pathos, lunacy and dark tragicomedy. Or it's as if life as the raw material of fiction is coarse-grained and you've refined it into a finesse of fineness. The only fiction that achieves a similar effect is Phil Dick's, but that doesn't detract from your distinctiveness. I guess it was, among other things, the sensitivity embedded — amidst its antithetical mental toughness — in your writing which first drew me to your work, and which I came to see mirrored in you personally.

Anyway, getting back to mundanities, my talk at the Jung Society, which to my surprise drew an audience of around 200, went over well and generated some lively discussion during question time, to the extent that I ended up sounding forth on sf as contemporary mythology. Someone then asked if there were any Oz sf writers worth reading, to which I replied, 'Yes! Now let's see there's.... (I'll leave the rest to your imagination.) This Thursday I'm scheduled to talk on a live radio show called 'The Metaphysical Hour' on Jung and the relationship between health and psychological wholeness.

I invited R to the UFO meeting last week and was relieved that he didn't turn up. The guy who spoke was embarrassingly incoherent and hearsayish; he had no concrete facts, or even pics of UFOism, just a lot of second-hand babble he'd picked up from self-proclaimed abductees. J F, who's speaking (on June 16) on 'sf before and after Tolkien', should be more reliable.

On the reading front, I've just finished Sterling's *Schismatrix*, a fascinating piece of near-dystopian posthumanism. Technologically, I found it richly inventive and intricately detailed, though I found it hard — owing perhaps to this maze of visual detail — to follow the plot (assuming there was one). The blur seemed to clear toward the end, though, when the main themes came more clearly into focus and the novel veered toward a final vision of transcendence, when the protagonist was transformed by 'the Presence' into his 'new self'. High points of the novel were the splendidly realised mimicking tape creature, and a giant sea scorpion living at -180 degrees C in a liquid ethane pool. The human dress styles reminded me of those in Russell B's 'Glass Reptile Breakout', while the aquatic genetics had some overlap with Zindell's in *Neverness*. All in all an expertly written and enjoyable read, though somewhat sexist in that the female characters are all unsubtly and aggressively seductive. Plus there were too many large, iridescent cockroaches whizzing about, which as a real situation would be for me the most nightmarish horror imaginable. Indeed, I've often dreamed of such garish scenes. And what does that tell me about *my* shadow, I wonder?

What you call your 'not-self' is of course what I mean by the disowned shadow, yours truly perhaps being, as I've hinted, a key embodiment of it for you. I hope this doesn't sound patronising, because it's not meant as such, but for a non-Jungian you're doing a bloody good job of bringing to light some buried material that needed to be dredged up from the darkness. I trust I'm doing an equally good job with my own blind spots. I have a confession to make, then. I intuitively sense in you an unquenchably strong drive toward wholeness and my guess is that it's increasingly asserting itself against the restraints of your conscious mind, a conflict which I felt clearly in my first Dream of you.

You've helped me beyond measure, through the courage and honesty, anger and compassion with which you've dealt with life as it is, in the finest way possible, by transposing it with brutal sensitivity into truthful art. Your imagination is truly Shakespearean, *mon ami*.

28 June 1995

Dear Phalange Fracturer

I was saddened to hear of your recent freak party-pooping pinky accident. I hope the finger's all mended again now? Come to think of it, flinging your arm recklessly 'into the heavens' disconcertingly brings to mind a certain well-known image of cultural crassness. I hope, in other words, that you weren't attempting a John Travolta simulation beneath flashing strobe lights, ironically to the tune of 'Staying Alive'? But of course I know you'd never do anything so distasteful. And what is one to do with a transparent plastic finger splint after it's served its prescribed purpose? Recycle it as a non-heatable test-tube, perhaps? Anyway, I hope there have been no further instances of corporeal ruin since your digit damaging.

The Mythopoeic evening (which I recently mentioned as forthcoming) was a success, in spite of poor attendance resulting from the publicist's negligent lack of publicising. F gave an entertaining overview of sf's development from Wells and Verne through to the influence of Gernsback, Campbell and other pre-Tolkieners, hence on to Cordwainer and other post-40s myth-makers. Plus he brought along an impressive selection of old magazines, including *Science Wonder Stories*, and *Unknown Worlds,* all featuring unintentionally hilarious illustrations of Brylcream-haired nerds diddling with dynamos and suchlike.

It was all immensely enjoyable and eventually turned into a debate-like, friendly free-for-all, which ended in a pleasant supper. The following Monday it was on to an arty party at M P's architecturally quirky hideaway. A visiting New York critic who writes for *Eidolon* and *NYRSF* was a guest, except that no-one seemed to want to talk to her, nor she to anyone else for that matter. I bravely gave it a go for about an hour but ended up doing about 90% of the talking. So after acquiring a headache through this mammoth effort I understood why F J had quietly declared (at the Mythopoeic meeting the Friday before) his intention of not turning up, because this lady was scheduled to be present. Still, I did manage to get out of her that she'd read most of your novels and criticism, and had heard you give a radio interview in which, according to her, you confessed that you wrote 'in order to be loved'.

Turning up at M P's home was like arriving at the threshold of a Hindu shrine, since we were asked to take off our shoes before entering the inner sanctum, in order to replace them with our choice of a pair of hand-knitted slippers for padding about in, perhaps in emulation of their ancient Siamese cat. I must say that T M looked rather quaint in his trendily crocheted, pointy-toed selection. I ended up spending most of the evening chatting amiably with Shane Dix and Sean Williams, who have just co-authored *The Unknown Soldier*, the first volume of their space opera-ish trilogy, due to be launched in a couple of weeks' time. Shane Dix and I spent some time chuckling over the numerous blunders and inconsistencies of *Trek*. On the ever-recurring subject of which you might have caught a few entertaining episodes of late, including the one where Worf zaps between parallel realities through a quantum rift in the spacetime continuum. Presumably, though, each Worf would theoretically be equally valid and totally ignorant of the others, so his final return in the episode to the one 'real' reality, via the conscious rejection of the others, struck me as an abuse of the 'parallel realities' theory. At the last Trekker day we watched the final (2-part) *TNG* episode, which sends the series out with a bang and is based on a tachyonic time regression paradox.

I was also intrigued, whilst talking shoelessly with M P and his wife, to discover that they're both regular attenders at the Jung Society — which is more than I am — which is why I've never seen them there. We then discussed plans for luring the blatantly archetypal Terry Dowling over to give a talk at said Society. M P also apologised profusely for missing my recent Jung talk, which provoked a string of appreciative phone calls, in particular one from a guy who's doing a maths PhD that draws in a fascinating way upon theories of mathematical archetypes and some of Penrose's ideas, though much of it goes over my head when he attempts to explain it. Unfortunately this guy lives in Gawler (about 50 km away) so can't readily drop around for a chat, but we've been having some enjoyable phone discussions. He's using ideas such as complex and imaginary numbers, plus morphic resonance in order to draw parallels with the ego/self axes and intersections. What's enthralling is that I used some of his key intuitions — spontaneous symmetry and self-ordering, for instance — in my thesis, so he's busily examining that at the moment. My radio talk also provoked some positive feedback, including phoned in comments that my views were refreshingly 'sane and balanced' in comparison with the usual stuff they get on this 'Metaphysical Hour', which I'd never tuned into before I spoke on it. Apparently they'd had someone channelling 'Ascended Masters' from the Pleiades on the previous week's show; not that I'm averse to such phenomena, but all too often these 'Masters' offer little more than dull platitudes, or spiritual 'insights' that we've already received, sometimes thousands of years ago, from mere Earthbound sages.

Returning to sf: we're currently organising a forum on the genre (in general) for the next Mythopoeic meeting in July, and this time we've decided to do the publicity ourselves, which should result in a sizeable audience. Bookwise, I've been absorbed in Tony Daniel's first novel, *Warpath*, which reads somewhat like a Red Indian version of Terry Dowling, with 'Wanderer' star captains levitating about the galaxy in Indian canoes, and a semi-sentient female weather algorithm which speaks in the guise of a wind. As well, I picked up at the local library Van Ikin's compact 'Portable Australian Authors' anthology, *Australian Science Fiction*, so I've got that — which includes your 'A Passage in Earth' — plus a pile of borrowed novels to look forward to. The other day I grabbed a brand new copy of *The Einstein Intersection* for $1 at a book sale. I've also just finished Peter Ackroyd's *The House of Doctor Dee*, a semi-horror tale connecting present-day London with the London of Renaissance magus John Dee. Needless to say I revelled in this one, since it's all about alchemy and related weirdness.

I'm now tracking down his other works, including *First Light*, a metaphysical extravaganza in which astronomer Damian Fall receives strange signals from the star Aldebaran.

I'm glad to hear your computer is up and running again. I've had to fork out around a week's wages for new batteries for my laptop. Your book news sounds disappointingly vague and evasive. Have you tried anyone else with *Theory* and *Transreality*? It's a pity that funding inevitably rears its ugly, hindering head, since both books strongly deserve to be published. What's happening with your Dog play? I hope I haven't missed it. Have you done any more with *White Abacus*? I must confess to having a hearty laugh at the *Reading By Silverfish* mistake; there must have been some sort of non-Freudian slip involved here, or maybe a cryptic Gnostic allusion, given that 'fishes' eyes' (*oculi piscium*) is a synonym for the alchemical 'scintillae', or 'soul-sparks' as (what Paracelsus calls) the 'stars' of the dark night sky of the soul. Hmm. The mind boggles like a goldfish's eyes.

I'd like to read the 'Overland' review of *Arch of Babel* which you mentioned. As for my book news, I've recently received an offer from Edwin Mellen Press (in Wales) to publish my Keats book, and they're not asking for money to do so. It'll be part of a series called the 'Salzburg University Studies Series Romantic Reassessment'. They don't pay royalties, but they do provide ten free copies, which is fine by me. I'd be happy just to see the thing in print.

On the psychotherapy front, I'm aiming gradually to ease myself out of teaching and into therapy more or less full-time. I've recently received considerable encouragement to do so, mainly from several practising Adelaide therapists, including a couple of guys who've been running a consultancy for about six years from their city office. They're both fairly keen to include a female partner for the sake of psychological balance, and as a result of recent discussions have offered to let me join their venture, which means I'll be able to use the office for 2–3 days per week. And the rent is pretty cheap for a city location.

The legal situation is that one can advertise oneself as a 'psychotherapist' but not as a 'Jungian analyst', since you can acquire the latter qualification only after coughing up a helluva lot of money to train at one of the Jung Institutes.

But side from financial considerations, psychotherapy needs to be embarked upon with caution, even trepidation and humility, since one is always exploring unknown seas when dealing with the unconscious, and therefore likely to learn at least as much as one is able to teach. A basic requirement of Jungian therapy is that it be a joint venture. There are no experts with all the answers; and we cannot guide another where we haven't been ourselves. The most one can do — and then only with the patient's cooperation — is help draw out the healing potential latent within the individual.

Perilous journeys into the depths of the psyche are more often than not undertaken alone, at least throughout the crucial stages of individuation that involve one's inner centre of gravity shifting from the ego to the consciously centred self. Strangely, or miraculously enough, I didn't end up at the funny farm as a result of my 1983–84 prolonged crucifixion between warring opposites. The closest I came was to visit a couple of friends who were temporary inmates — not that being there did them much good — plus at one time I was running music therapy sessions at a Psychiatric Hospital, during which I occasionally got into hair-raising discussions about God and His cohorts with various prophesying patients.

I've felt drawn to practising therapy for around 10 years, but it's never 'felt right' on a level deeper than the ego until recently. Now it's like I'm being firmly yet gently lured and prodded into it, since it's certainly not something to be undertaken lightly, rashly, or egotistically. But of course the deciding factor for success or failure will be whether I can actually help anyone. If anyone tells me that I've harmed them, or I ever get to feeling that I'm no longer doing any good, I'll back off at once. So far, though, the responses have been encouraging, so I'll proceed with caution and see where and to whom it leads.

You mention that you've been watching 'Passions of the Soul' on SBS again. I agree with you that one is on dodgy ground when attempting strictly to apply — as Pauli's former therapist did — psychological causes to physical illnesses such as cancer. Who knows, Pauli is just as likely to have contracted smoking-induced lung cancer, or low fibre-induced bowel cancer. Still, the series does cover some useful ground, particularly in the field of reinterpreting religion in psychological terms.

If your programming's the same in Melbourne, you may have noted that the series has been sensibly preceded by the superb 'Joseph Campbell and the Power of Myth' documentaries, given that of all mythologists, Campbell is ideologically closest to Jung. I taped both shows when they were first screened but have been watching them this time round, too. My favourite 'Passions' episode, which was on last week, featured interviews with two remarkable women whom I admire and respect for their wisdom, quiet strength, compassion and outstanding courage in the face of personal tragedy; indeed, they've been favourite role models for me for years. I refer to the Gnostic bishop Elaine Pagels (Professor of Comparative Religion), and Blake scholar and Jungian analyst, June Singer.

While I'm writing this, ABC-FM is airing a show full of music from well-known sf movies, such as *Logan's Run*. The oven is baking bizarre-looking cheese straws. I hope you're staying warm and cosy. As for me, I'll soon be off to bed to read, with my trusty hot water bottle in tow.

18 July 1995

Dear Damien

Not much news from my neck of the woods. In fact it's more a case of wood of the neck, which I've recently gained considerable relief from by swapping therapies with a couple of fascinating women I've met, one who does Neuroskeletal Dynamics and the other reflexology and massage, for which I gratefully exchange dreamwork and art therapy sessions. Alas, it's all the result of my riveted absorption in books and computer screens, which of course you'd also know a lot about, but what is one to do with a heart and soul that can't stop restlessly questing for truth and wonder in whatever guises they choose to reveal themselves? Sadly, though, I usually end up hovering quantum-like amidst a haze of possibilities rather than actualities, since the weakness of intuitives is their reluctance to commit themselves to any one thing, for fear of losing sight of the whole picture and other endless possibilities, most of which, therefore, seldom materialise.

This is where I've learnt so much from you, since you at least manage to get things done, and done extremely well in the bargain. Reading through *Dreaming Dragons* again has left me wondering how you managed to write that marvellous passage where the Soul Core is entered through the ten circles of light. Here you beat Dowling to the literary use of crystals! I might add that your sense of progression through the visible spectrum toward the X-rays outside the central singularity is nothing short of a stroke of genius.

I enjoyed your review of some books in the latest *Weekend Australian.* In terms of overlapping themes you linked the four books together marvellously, and I was left wanting to rush out and buy them all — another goal which didn't eventuate — this time due to a lack of cash. As you clarify, subverting Descartes from all sorts of angles is undoubtedly the name of the game in current trends of scientific thought. I felt that the rather silly image accompanying the review was an unfortunate editorial choice, however. Your radio interview last week on ABC was equally absorbing. Although the interviewer's questions weren't particularly well put, you acquitted yourself with your customary eloquence, intelligence and wit, plus your tales about your youthful years threw some light on the deep extent to which your Catholic background has influenced you.

I just received two rejections for teaching jobs I applied for a few months back; one (in English) at Uni of Queensland, the other (in Language Skills) at Uni of Newcastle. Such dullness aside, I've been in hibernation mode for most of this winter; reading, writing, meditating, sleeping like a dormant bulb. I suppose that to most folk my life would seem outwardly unspectacular, even uneventful, though the view from within is always anything but. Apart from sifting through numerous CD-ROMs and scouting about in libraries, I've been preparing my next round of sf talks for the Uni course, running a course on active imagination and dreams at a Community Centre, doing some one to one dreamwork, and fussing about with attempts to revise contracts for copyright permissions for my Keats book from Harvard and Cambridge UPs. I pleaded with them to take into account that I stand to make no financial gain from the venture, so I hope they don't slog me too much for their wretched permissions. It's ironic that they profit from owning the rights to the letters and poems of a guy who made nix out of them himself, but then such has been the usual lot of impoverished, struggling artists who in their own lifetime don't get the recognition they deserve. (Does this ring a faint bell?) It sounds like Liverpool UP could be a goer for your *Transreality*, even if they won't be paying. I hope you've had more definite responses to other ventures, though, notably the US follow-up to *Lotto Effect*.

I've just received an invite from The Wagner Society to give a talk on archetypes in the 'Ring' cycle, so I'm currently steeling myself to study a 15 hour video series of said opera.

I've also been running a Wednesday evening discussion group at my place for about seven folk I recently encountered, who are all keen to delve more into dream analysis, myths, science, sf and Jung. I've just been reading Penrose's *Emperor's*

New Mind again as a basis for some possible group discussions on contemporary Platonism. I must say it's a darned nuisance that we can at best remember 20% of what we read, and when such poor economy is further undermined by an Easternish tendency to unclutter the mind, one feels doomed endlessly to reread, which in my case often feels like pouring water into a sieve. But at least a few drops — hopefully pertinent pearls of wisdom — always manage to cling to the surface.

I've lined up an sf forum for this Friday's Mythopoeic group, which will take the form of N R firing hopefully answerable questions at a panel of four, comprising Sean Williams, Dr Haydn Williams (no relation), myself and Peter Delin (hey — a 3+1 quaternity!). I've also put together some video clips to highlight comparisons between *The Martian Chronicles* and a 1926 Russian sf film, *Aelita,* a melodramatic rigmarole about the Martian equivalent of the 1917 Revolution. The Martian sets and costumes are impressive, nonetheless, but the main connection with Bradbury is that a Martian lady arouses her lover's jealousy by falling in love with an Earth guy she tunes into with visual telepathy.

I haven't seen the PhD maths scholar for a couple of weeks, since he's been in Melbourne doing some research. He's dropped round a couple of times to exchange news and reading matter, so I did finally get to meet him in person. He's a fascinating guy, but I wouldn't exactly call him a kindred spirit, and even though we share a zestful intellectual rapport, in response to your query about possible 'romantic interest', no, my heart is not drawn to him the way it has been to you. I love you for who you are, not because you conform to my ideals, or agree with me. Besides, those who share my insights only reinforce what I already know, and you surely know by now how much I thrive on the creative challenge of opposition.

Did you catch Paul Davies being interviewed in the outback about the Big Bang by Phillip Adams on SBS last Sunday night?

They obviously forgot to bring along the Aerogard. Still, the series promises some worthwhile viewing, particularly as they loom ever closer to the 'Big Question', presumably about 'God' and the meaning of life. Should that eventuate, let's hope their answer to it all isn't '42'.

Why don't you treat yourself to a well-deserved holiday in the US? Apart from being an ideal escape from winter, it might be just the thing to inspire you to launch into *The White Abacus*. Of course my reasons for encouraging you to keep on with it include the selfish one of wanting to read it! Ta muchly for sending over the Dowling book, by the way. I've only read the intro so far and was pleasantly amused by his dabblings into crystal lore. Since I've got at least half of the stones he names, I'll keep them on hand, or perhaps balance them over the Third Eye as I read the corresponding tales (just kidding.) Speaking of Intimate Knowledge of the Night, it's time to fill the hot water bottle again. I often sit at my desk with it propped gurglingly against my back, which is good for inducing me to sit upright.

So what do I lie awake and ponder at night? I've been mooning – perhaps as a form of lunacy – over a moon; I mean a moon of Uranus, Miranda. I relish in these free holidays, courtesy of the imagination. The other night I was watching a video on the outer planets, enthralled by photos of rings and storms, when suddenly a NASA guy came on pointing to a blow-up of a 16-mile-high mountain range on Miranda, while he casually remarked that it would take 8 minutes for a stone thrown from the top to hit the ground, allowing for gravity specifics. There was something eerily thrilling about him pointing to these mountains, owing partly, I suppose, to the realisation that they (presumably) have remained unobserved for billions of years and now in some sense, even if only via technology, have at last been seen. I kept freeze-framing the photo image because the landscape evoked that most awesome and tingling of emotions: the sense of the sublime. More than anything else I wanted to be there, amid the frozen, dim, airless, lone and silent stillness of the valley below, gazing up at those mountains. Then I began to entertain ideas for a story in which a huge finger appears in the actual sky of Miranda, thereby replicating the video image of the guy pointing to the photo. The challenge would be to provide a plausible rationale and reason for the giant finger appearing. All very PhilDickian — perhaps a short story version could be called 'Finger in the Sky'.

21 August 1995

Dear Damien

I hope you've had good news from publishers and that you're staying healthy. Life wasn't meant to be wheezy, or was it? I suppose you're gearing up for the September Writers Festival in Queensland? It should provide you with an enjoyable break and some stimulating interaction with fellow artists.

Last Thursday night at the Uni of Adelaide, amidst considerable media hype and to a keen crowd of thousands, Paul Davies gave a guest lecture on SETI and the self-organising universe. He ended on an appropriately musical note, by playing that well-known Monty Python number about the immensity of the cosmos and the lack of intelligent life on Earth. Needless to say, this brought the house down. I brought my brother along, since as a result of my corrupting influence he's recently become an avid reader of Davies and Hawking, so was keen to get his latest Davies purchase autographed in the foyer afterwards. I joined in and while we were chatting away about faces and pyramids on Mars, Paul brought forth from his pocket a genuine Martian rock — part of a meteorite discovered by Mawson — which I was allowed to examine at leisure. Paul warned me not to put it out of sight, though. Apparently security guards were on hand, ready to pounce on anyone trying to pilfer the rock. I must say it did feel kind of magical holding this stone, knowing it had zipped across space from another world. It was black and shiny, sort of like a cross between obsidian and coal. My day was made, and eventually and reluctantly I handed it back. Somewhere along the line I also mentioned to Paul that you'd dropped by to see him when you were over here last year.

On a more personal note, I'm sad that our differing takes on reality have triggered a defensive hostility on your part, though I sensed that things might eventually erupt in this way, and that it might be a necessary development, however painful, if certain truths were ever to come to light, so by no means have I taken your negative reaction to heart. As I've made clear before, I know better than to fight against an all-powerful archetype, in this case your anima reinforced by the subversive power of your rejected shadow. As Jung says, we idealise whenever there is a secret fear to be exorcized, and what is feared is usually the unconscious and its 'magical' influence. Hence your doubly reactionary response to me as a representative of both your 'not-self' foe, and your 'not-mother' in the bargain.

We're responsible only for the harm we intentionally commit. While we remain unaware of our projections, they have total power over us and we're doomed to follow the carrot they dangle before us, because the archetype in itself can never be fully realised in any one person. The best we can manage is to find a temporary carrier of its all-powerful energy, until the spell weakens and we're forced to seek elsewhere *ad infinitum* for our elusive ideal.

I hesitate to write any of this because it seems that whatever I say, or do only further exacerbates the tension between us. But as always, I follow my heart and intuition in such matters, and since it feels right to be writing this today, I'll proceed ramblingly and see where it leads. I'd never compromise my honesty toward you, Damien, even if it means — as apparently it already has — losing your affection and respect. The therapist's task is often a thankless one, even to the extent of sometimes generating outright hatred in the 'patient'. In fact as I've already learned, it's delicate work, sort of like extracting a resisting worm from its safe darkness. If you tug too hard the worm breaks and all is lost. If, on the other hand, you make no effort at all, the situation may remain in darkness. It's a tricky and potentially hazardous business, a meandering journey throughout which one becomes increasingly aware of one's own blind spots, neuroses and preconceptions, thereby able to appreciate why Jung, when asked what he thought held the 'four functions' of consciousness together, replied, 'a sense of humour'. In the end, what matters most is the human quality, since ultimately the therapist IS the therapy.

But apart from a perhaps worthwhile clearing up of certain misunderstandings, above the superficial noise of your annoyance I hear what I've all along sensed to be coming from you: the cry of a man desperately at war with himself, though I needn't elaborate on what you're more aware of than I ever could be. Other than that, you know by now that like you, I'm not entirely lacking in self-criticism. We can ill afford to be at any time, yet alone when attempting to help others come to terms with their difficulties. Do you honestly believe that I'd ever resort to offering glib advice to a person of your sensibility, intelligence, depth and scope of character, particularly when I've all along been aware that I stand to learn as much from you as you possibly could from me? In describing how I experience life, I can't improve on what has already been said by another, namely that a 'religious person is devout in the sense that [she] has no doubt of the significance of those superpersonal objects and goals which neither require nor are capable of rational foundation'. Source of quote? Albert Einstein.

As I recall, I made it clear some time ago that there's no such thing as a 'license' to practice as a Jungian therapist. Jung's approach is at odds with that of more 'reputable' schools, all of which rely heavily on techniques, convenient categorisations, theories, objectivity, and the 'myth' of the therapist's expertise. But are you really prepared to dismiss me on the strength of a jestingly included magazine clipping and a light-hearted quip about Dowling and his nocturnal stones? Of course, as we've noted before, we've each been guilty of taking the other too seriously at times. If, after all I've shared with you, you find it so easy to lump me in indiscriminately with the kinds of New Agers you abhor, then I'm sorry for your sake that such a misunderstanding persists. I've wrongly assumed that at some stage you came to realise that I'm as annoyed as you are by obsequious and puerile individuals who plagiarise ancient spiritual teachings, then regurgitate them as New Age enlightenment.

For the record, the ad was placed in that particular publication not because I uncritically condone its content, but because the folk who read it are more likely to be open to holistic therapies, and Jung's is the only paradigm of the psyche that fits the bill. And I don't recall ever claiming that crystals have 'magical' properties. I collect them because I find them fascinating and beautiful, as I do countless other natural phenomena — planets, stars, moons, snowflake mandalas, mushrooms, trees and 7-hearted earthworms — by virtue of their quintessential mystery and uniqueness. Whatever helpful energies crystals have most likely arise from their being an instance of the 'spirit in matter', a genuinely Aquarian Age phenomenon that transcends the obsolete Piscean dualism of matter and spirit.

Your concern for my potential victims is touching, but I assure you they're in no danger of being offered patronising 'advice' of any kind. In fact your assumptions about psychotherapy are out of alignment with how it actually works, if and when it does. I don't know where you got your ideas about psychotherapy from, but I assure you they're completely misguided. But don't take my word for it. If you're at all curious to know what Jung's views on the matter are, you might care to look at his *CW* Vol. 16, 'The Practice of Psychotherapy'. I'd be happy to send you copies of a couple of chapters if you can't get hold of the book. But since I made a big effort to clarify all this a few letters ago, I can only assume you've either forgotten, ignored, or discredited what I wrote.

Thanks as well for your honest criticism along other, more personal lines, but I assure you I'm more aware of my many flaws than you are. On the physical front, short of neurotically striving for perfection, like many folk, yourself included, I do what I can to stay healthy and improve myself, for my own sake. But neither of us is getting any younger, and a slowing metabolism unfortunately often translates into a few unwanted pounds, especially for us women. Ironically, I found your physical imperfections — not that I've ever viewed them in this light — endearing rather than repellent, and I would only wish them altered or removed in instances where they were causing you physical suffering, or harm in some way.

I have no wish to argue with you, Damien, since I feel it would only aggravate your antagonism further. Plus it would only add fuel to your conviction of being a lone individual battling against a largely deluded world, when you know as well as I do that the real enemy (your 'not-self foe') lurks defiantly within you. Thus at least as I see it, a vital factor in your future growth will be whether you'll remain determined to cast your shadow everywhere except where it rightfully belongs, namely within yourself; or as Jung incisively puts it:

> *When we allow ourselves to be irritated out of our wits by something, let us not assume that the cause of our irritation lies simply and solely outside us, in the irritating thing or person. In that way we endow them with the power to put us into a state of irritation, and possibly even one of insomnia or indigestion. We then turn round and unhesitatingly condemn*

the object of offence, while all the time we are raging against an unconscious part of ourselves which is projected onto the exasperating object.
[*Dreams*, 1974, p. 57]

Exchanging shadow-fuelled, verbal crossfire with you doesn't meet my criteria for an amiable, mutually respectful and worthwhile relationship. Short of absurdly apologising for being who I am, I feel I've done all I can to meet you half way, by accepting the equal validity of your own take on life. My crime, it seems, has been to offer you support and friendship through sharing with you how I experience and view life, and encouraging you to do precisely the same.

I'm not sure whether you're still open to sharing news and views and mutual interests, so perhaps I'd best not ramble on any further. I feel uncomfortable writing defensively to you when I've only ever wished to communicate on mutually affectionate grounds. Regardless of the outcome of this letter, then, I shall always think kindly toward and highly of you and, should you ever need me as such, I shall always remain your friend.

20 September 1995

Dear Dr Day (a character in one of Dowling's tales)

You're right of course, there are legitimate irritations and only ruthless honesty with oneself can distinguish them from genuine shadow problems. Even highly revered souls get irritated, as was Christ by the Pharisees, Gandhi by the British, Jung by the dolts who labelled him as a charlatan. It's not my place to tell you what your shadow projections are; you've already demonstrated that you're discerning enough to figure that out for yourself, so I apologise for insulting your integrity in such an underhanded way.

Like it or not — and I know you don't — life is about harmonising opposing energies and eventually it will demand that of both of us.

I've never claimed that the physical side of relationships doesn't matter, only that there's something which ultimately matters more and which over time can grow rather than fade. Surely an overemphasis of sex is just as imbalanced as shunning it. There are usually two sides to an issue and I heartily agree that we can use immunity to criticism as an excuse for making no attempt to improve ourselves. But in the longterm there's no stopping entropy and the flow of time, and eventually in any lasting relationship factors other than sex come to the fore, or all is lost. Maybe I'm wrong to assume that this compassionate kind of love could ever mean something to you; if it couldn't then you won't understand what I've tried repeatedly to convey. I find it hard to accept, though, that somewhere within you, beyond your yearning for romantic adventure, there isn't an even deeper longing to be loved in a more simple, enduring and human way. By all means tell me if I'm wrong. Besides, isn't it possible that your obsession with sex — your view of it as opposed to 'spirit' rather than as an expression of it — is a rebellion against the flesh-hating repressiveness of Catholicism, and therefore equally unbalanced?

Last year you seemed more open to welcoming our differences, even learning from them. Why else, for instance, would you have taken Wolff's 4-fold sequence into account as a possible template for your own life's unfolding pattern? Before you came to visit me you already knew what my take on life was and you seemed open to the possibility of having a close relationship with a Wolffian 'medium', even though you were aware that such beings have in turn a close relationship with the collective unconscious. If you hadn't at least been open to acknowledging the validity of my reality, on what grounds did you decide that you wanted to spend time with me? How in gods' names could a Jungian 'medium' not be different from, or in some way complementary to you? What saddens me is that you've exaggerated the importance of physical factors to the extent that whatever positive qualities I do have to offer seem to be of comparatively little value to you. At the very least I've offered you friendship, emotional support and intellectual companionship, but you're not an easy man to love, Damien, not because you're unlovable but because you won't allow yourself to be loved.

All the men I was involved with before you were conventionally good-looking as well as, personality-wise, idealised versions of my idolised father, and as I've mentioned before, part of my breaking free from this complex has come through finally learning to love a man who's not in the least like my dad, so perhaps I've made some progress. While I was growing up dad and I spent a lot of time sharing common loves: art, music, writing, astronomy, calligraphy and photography, so the idea of sexual love for me has always included the necessity of shared passions. I guess I hoped that you'd be someone with whom I could share a joint need to be enriched and inspired by such loves. But I mistakenly assumed that such an overlap of interests would be equally important — maybe even more important than physical parameters — to you. In the end, we must each remain true to ourself.

One difference between us is that whereas I've always been fond of you in spite of, maybe even because of your weaknesses, my flaws seem to have eroded whatever simple affection you might at one time have felt toward me. I've never judged, or condemned your emotional paralysis and self-loathing, nor would I ever do so. I prefer to see such symptoms as psychic wounds rather than as deliberate sins of omission or commission, and as such they tend to respond more readily to compassion than to criticism. Certainly in my own experience it's those who are wounded — and who have found the gifts hidden in their wounds — who make the best healers. Someone who's convinced they have no weaknesses or problems would make a far less effective, even potentially harmful therapist, which is where the Wounded Healer archetype comes into play.

Alas, there seems to be little room for simple human warmth in your life. Maybe during your strict Catholic upbringing you were deprived of such gifts as a child; I don't know. I'm not trying to ascribe blame, merely trying to cast a gentle light on areas of deep woundedness which, as you probably realise yourself, remain unresolved. What may have seemed to you like unresponsiveness on my part was triggered by my picking up on your emotional barriers and resistance to the warmth and affection I wanted to give you. I felt apologetic about offering you even simple gestures of fondness.

Being offended is all too often a defensive rationalisation against accepting the truth, however painful and however blatantly it might be presented. While criticism, however constructive, has its uses, inner wounds are ultimately healed through self-love, non-judgmental acceptance by another, patience and understanding, along with a healthy dose of humour when it's called for. To be a helpful therapist one needs not only honesty toward oneself, but also kindness, empathy, and a heart-centred ability to be a receptive vessel who cradles the cauldron in which the alchemy of mutual transformation unfolds.

As far as your misgivings about my psychotherapy work goes, I'm sorry that you find it necessary to assume the worst. I'm aware of five therapists practising in Adelaide, not one of whom (myself included) is the least bit interested in 'fucking with people's heads in a mock therapeutic setting', or setting up marketplace shingles as lone operators. That's why we meet each week to discuss problems, offer feedback on each other's work, and arrange to exchange therapy. Yes indeedy, the therapists need to be analysed too; Jung insisted on it and so do we. After all, it's the blockages and blind spots therapists remain unconscious of that are likely to prove hazardous in therapeutic situations.

If other women you've been involved with have been temperamentally and ideologically like you, then perhaps you've never had the chance to appreciate other approaches to sexuality. I, for one, love deeply or not at all, and sex for me has always been inseparable from love, by which I don't simply mean romantic intoxication. I don't think there's anything particularly strange or unusual about this attitude; in fact many women I've known have shared the same emotional values. Do you really believe, for instance, that verbal quirkiness, sardonicism, athleticism — plus other traits you've listed as desirable in women — are more admirable qualities than simple human kindness, gentleness, loyalty and affection? And don't retort by going on about 'compatibility' when your past relationships, which presumably were based on your 'admirable' criteria, have for one reason or another all failed. Are you willing to face what lies behind these attempts to make yourself more attractive, or likeable as a substitute for accepting that you already are? Isn't attracting the 'interest' of women you're 'interested' in the same as promoting mutually conditional acceptance, rather than unconditional love? And what will happen when you reach a time when you can no longer command sufficient sexual presence to attract any interest? You'll then either have to remain alone, or accept someone's unconditional love for you.

I know your Catholic background, reinforced by your father's rejection of you, has instilled into you the conviction that you're unworthy, worthless and sinful, but that's all a bigger load of bulldust than any New Age hocus pocus. For all its proneness to naïveté, at least the better aspects of the latter focus on healing, sensitivity to Nature and self-acceptance. Another thing that irritates me about you is your presumption that science *per se* is antagonistic to New Age thought, when you know as well as

I do that scientists, like the rest of us, are by and large divided into two camps: holists (Penrose, Davies, Bohm, Pribham, Jung, Pauli, Bohr) and materialists (Dawkins and his ilk).

Anyway, whatever I've been in the past, I'm certainly not 'remote' from my body at the moment. I've been getting myself into shape not to please someone else, or to attract sexual interest, but because it feels great and makes me more content, focused, calm, and healthier to do so. My self-improving spree has included (in one week) a body massage, a facial, a cellulite treatment, a visit to the hairdresser, and guzzling 12 glasses of spring water per day in order to detoxify and hydrate. So far this new regimen is having encouraging results. To tell you the truth, I feel pretty damned good about myself at the moment. My health is fine, my energy levels are higher, my skin is glowing and I feel at least ten years younger.

So yes, we're each emotionally crippled in different ways. So why not try to help each other? Not all wounds can, or should be healed and maybe you need yours to be as potent and distinctive a writer as you are. Anyway, I wanted to take the time to be more honest and open with you, to share something of a new level of awareness that's been subtly filtering into my life, however corny or mystical that might sound, and to thank you for prodding me into deeper self-evaluation.

Bless you, Dayananda. Take care.

1 November 1995

Dear Damien

Thanks for your letter's news and views. It sounds as though we've both been indulging in the usual feast of reading and wondering about the meaning of it all. I've been wading through a smorgasbord of stuff by various sages and scientists, including the Dalai Lama, who seems pretty cluey about physics, Prigogine on chaos theory and the creative arrow of time (as opposed to the idea of a static, hidden order), Lama Govinda on the plenum-void, Hawking on whether or not there's an edge to the universe, Bohm on the super-implicate order and on matter as a meaning field, Rupert Sheldrake on morphogenetic fields (almost the same thing as archetypes), and Krishnamurti, whom I'm gravely suspicious of, since he rejects science outright and hubristically claims never to have learned anything from anybody.

Sheldrake's ideas overlap with Bohm's, since as you probably already know he proposes a sort of Darwin/Plato hybridisation, through which morphic fields through resonance evolve as a result of the cumulative feedback of past and present forms. Interestingly, in contrast to Bohm and Sheldrake, who comfortably straddle both mysticism and scientific holism, Krishnamurti and Hawking are absolutist opposites — Hawking with an extreme positivist view of Nature as that which contains no mysteries but only puzzles that will eventually yield to equations — and Krishnamurti who, with equal minimalism, claims that only the noumenal matters. Hawking seeks the first moment when time emerged from the timeless void, while K claims he's found the ending of time. For H the key to the puzzle of being is time, for K it is timelessness. Each is vehement and passionate in his stand, and each pursues it to the exclusion of everything else. Each has integrity, purity of focus, high intelligence, and love for one view of reality. Both are creators, not followers. Still, who knows, it seems likely that the answer to the Big Question will come from neither of them. But it's rewarding to delve into it all, as I'm sure you'll agree.

I recently had a birthday, by the way, which was commemorated with a family feast at the local Indian restaurant — which isn't called 'Milliways'. I've been doing other reasonably absorbing activities, as I trust you have. I ran a workshop on active imagination at an alternative medicine convention last weekend. About 60 people turned up and even though no money was involved, it was an opportunity for some free publicity for my psychotherapy practice, out of which I'm currently not making a living, since whatever I earn goes straight back into advertising. Still, I'm getting some valuable experience from interacting closely with people and have had some tough challenges to work through, such as the manic depression and suppressed memory of a suspected child abuse victim, a dope addict who's determined to quit, and a woman who keeps dreaming that her head is falling off.

I've also been doing voluntary work for the local Women's Community Centre, where I'm also offering cheap and/or free therapy sessions for those who are struggling financially. Next door to the Women's Centre is Radio Station 3D, who've offered me a regular talkback spot during which I attempt to answer questions from letters people have sent in the week before. Usually they're about dreams. I might also be getting a free plug on Channel Nine's 'Adelaide Today' show since I've volunteered to do a short interview for them. Aside from these goings on, I'm still dithering about with my Keats book, trying to organise a preface, plus renewing copyright permissions. Still, I'm pleased that it's been accepted for publication, and as a Celtic soul I'm happier having a Welsh publisher than I would have been with UP of America.

Your recently enjoyed Maudlin (what a depressing name!) book on quantum non-locality sounds like a worthwhile read. I'll see if I can track it down. Why did T unfairly regard *R By S* as 'a disappointing book'? I'm sorry to hear that the Uni of Liverpool Press rejected your *Transrealism* book; have you sent it elsewhere since? How far have you got with *White Abacus*? I'm also sorry to hear that the blue-rinse set dominated your Warana audience. I'm sure that whatever you had to say deserved a more varied, appreciative and larger audience.

Speaking of rinses, I recently dyed my hair dark red using pure henna powder (no chemicals, just pulverised stems and leaves which form a kind of lumpy mud when mixed with hot water). Needless to say it was fun applying this, washing it out an hour later, then scrubbing the bathroom to get rid of the considerable mess. Anyway, the upshot is that my lighter strands of hair have, in contrast to the darker shading, taken on an ominous, blood red hue. Still, it feels pleasant, though a trifle vampirish, to have a change.

I'm writing a talk on Jung and science for the Jung Society and hope to economise by presenting the same talk, with minor modifications, to the Theosophical Society, a broad-minded bunch who hold stimulating weekly discussion evenings and avoid pushing any particular religion, or dogma.

The Mythopoeic Society here looks like it might be folding up at the end of this year, partly because we've run out of funds, but mainly because the Committee has never been able to get its act together in terms of individual members actually making an effort to keep the thing afloat. The lion's share of responsibility for publicity, booking of speakers and venues, finances and correspondence, has consequently fallen repeatedly to Haydn Williams and me, such that we've both recently declared that we've had enough and are heartily sick of doing all the work. Anyway, the AGM will be held in a few weeks' time and if the Society decides to fold I intend to propose that we use the remaining funds to purchase some sf novels and donate them to the Barr Smith Library. I've heard on the grapevine, incidentally, that a big Mythopoeic Conference is scheduled for the year 2000 in Brisbane, where it all began some 12 years ago.

To end on an entirely different note, now that the next F1 Grand Prix is looming, I'm starting to get a knot in my stomach again. I can't explain it, but the death of Ayrton Senna pierced my soul with a deep wound that refuses to heal, or even form a scar. I'm wondering whether my soul somehow bonded to his while my consciousness was with him in the Dream when he died. I know it sounds pretty weird and you're probably being pushed way out of your comfort zone just by reading this. But I need to share this constant ache with someone. An analyst would most likely try to explain it all solely in terms of my own psyche, but who knows, there may be more to it than that. I've certainly never felt anything remotely like this about anyone else. On May 1 this year I lit a candle and meditated for hours, in remembrance of the day he died in Italy last year.

I once met Tolkien in a dream, in which we chatted about fantasy and myth as we strolled back at sunset from a Cambridge lecture he'd just given. But that was a 'small d' dream. With Ayrton, it was emotionally like a mountain falling into the sea and forming tidal waves that radiate outward through time, with no diminishment of their size. It's a strangely peaceful energy, though, as long as I 'go with the flow' of it. When I do, I experience an inseparable blend of wonderment and deep sorrow. Enough said.

29 November 1995

Dear Actually Scribbling Skiffy Skribbler

Glad to hear your novel is well underway. Thanks for the intriguing synopsis and Magic Beanstalk info.

Rather than suggestions, I have questions.

Are your catapults and ram accelerators cryptic allusions to Shakespeare's 'slings and arrows of outrageous fortune'?

Is your hero prone to long soliloquies concerning the pros and cons of existing?

Clarke's space-elevator theme has of course been done to death. What struck me blatantly is that it's one almighty phallic symbol: 'a stream of projectiles is shot up the bore of a hollow tower' (p. 63). Further on: 'A Space Fountain does not have to go straight up. The projectiles from the base station could be sent off in an angle in a large partial-orbital arc....' (p. 73). Hmm. I was always pretty hopeless at maths and physics so can't offer any constructive feedback on the theoretical front. The best I can do is to drop a copy of your letter into Paul Davies' office, along with a note asking if he can recommend any colleagues, or postgrads here or in Melbourne who might be willing to be on hand for advice while you're completing the book.

I agree that a dull old rocket is certainly not the way to get T back into orbit and the projectile method sounds a bit convoluted and clumsy. Why not use a tractor-beam powered by the gravitational field of a pulsar, or preferably, in order to fool the anti-teleportationists, T's life-sized hologram is somehow projected into space.

What about including, as a red herring, a swine of a character named Nocab?

As a bonus, following up on this idea — and since T's dad has been killed — the ghostly father factor could be spliced in. It works like this: the hologram projector is faulty and causes the image sporadically to fluctuate and waver into the semblance of a spirit. One of the reincarnation religion mob runs into the faulty image, mistakes it for T's dead dad, confronts it and using a direct quote from *Hamlet* Act One, says, 'I'll cross it, though it blast me'. You could get even more mileage out of the hologram idea by having it and the real T developing as alter egos of one another.

As an ecologically viable alternative to mining metals, what about proposing some sort of weird yet technically feasible alchemy. Maybe you could have a rival sect of secretive, subversive alchemists to annoy the hell out of the orthodox reincarnationists. Here you could work in Hamlet's query, 'And yet, to me, what is this quintessence of dust?' But enough of such stuff and nonsense. Seriously though, I'm truly pleased that you've moved into writerly mode and I eagerly anticipate receiving actual chunks of text soon.

All I can say is that your ideas sound neither stupid nor unsound, but beyond that I'm hardly qualified to comment. In fact, some of the problems you pose read like questions one might put to a TV 'Mastermind' panel with an average IQ of 200. For gods' sake, though, don't stifle your feminine sensitivity and allow the whole thing to get bogged down in technobabble. I know from your past work that you're unlikely to let this happen, but be reminded that your sensitivity to the human dilemma is a major ingredient of your special magic as a writer.

The Mythopoeic Society has calcified into a bunch of old and middle-aged fuddy-duddies who are more interested in discussing where an unaccounted for $2 has gone than in pondering the wonders of life, the universe and everything. Not that age *per se* has anything to do with it, but I've got better things to do than stifle yawns at meetings concerned solely with committee structures and policies.

Lately I've been delving into Marie-Louise von Franz's profound insights into alchemy. By the way, do you still have that neo-alchemical tape which you mentioned a few months back? If you have, would you mind posting it over? I'd send it back once I've had a listen. Naturally I mainly want to find out how to refine gold and levitate – useful tricks which would circumvent both monetary and mobility restrictions.

Meanwhile life leaps and limps along as best it can. I've been getting more lessons on How To Write through reading Dan Simmons' *Fires of Eden,* a Hawaiian-based horror tale about Mark Twain and a couple of spunky women battling a giant, 8-eyed pig god who's the enemy of the volcano goddess. Also, I've been contemplating the possibility of attending the second Oz Conference on 'Jungian Psychology and Spirituality' to be held in January in Melbourne, but the registration fee is hefty, so I'll probably give it a miss. Looks like I'll have to make do with the Theosophical Society Conference, to be held at Adelaide Uni around the same time, and the registration fee's only $40 for 6 days.

I've finally resigned as President of the Mythopoeic Society. Instead I intend to pour more energy into running weekend workshops on sf, science and myth for the Jung Society, plus I'm offering 2 Adelaide Uni courses next year, one on 'sf and science' and the second on 'Jung and creativity'.

Other minor news is that Prof. Rob White, a well-known Keats scholar, has kindly offered to provide a Preface for my book, which I'm of course pleased about. I've also been studying visionary and performance art, and reading up on Druidic animal shamanism, mainly because I've been dreaming that I'm a Druid shaman. In one recent vivid dream I was performing a healing ritual by dancing clockwise around a prone patient, whilst wielding a live serpent familiar and singing an intensely emotional chant in fluent Gaelic. All in a day's (or night's) work.

Anyway, I'm off to bed, perchance to dream.

1996 Letters

3 January 1996

Dear Damien

I was thrilled to hear that you've finished the first draft of *White Abacus*. Has it been accepted in advance for publication and if so by whom? You must have been at it pretty solidly for the past few months to have clocked up such an impressive word count. Well done indeed, and I hope you feel as proud of yourself as you have every right to feel. You mention including borrowed letter text. I like the idea of being an 'Absent Interlocutor' in the novel, seeing as the consciousness of 'being in the midst of non-being' has always appealed to me as a self-styled mystic. What's the current status of the two other novels you've co-authored with Rory?

Did you receive that AI dictionary I mentioned to you on New Year's Eve? I'm glad the Aldiss collection was an appropriate gift. I've just finished reading one of his older short story collections, *Last Orders*. A few of his offbeat inventions reminded me of certain offspring of Cordwainer's even more bizarre imagination. Another striking idea (in 'The Aperture Moment') was Aldiss's Cordwainer-like prophesying about homeopathic finches which flew about opening coloured shutters, beneath which numbers were revealed in a meaningful order.

As I nostalgically review the past year, aside from more pragmatic concerns I've been musing over how much I feel I've changed and (hopefully) grown and outgrown, largely as a result of the kinds of challenges you've presented me with. Along these lines, the following quote, lifted from von Franz's lectures on the psychology of alchemy, recently struck me as relevant to the kind of mutual need that has perhaps helped to fuel the ongoing dynamic between you and me. But can you relate to it, too?

> *Inordinate passion seeks defeat. People who have an inordinately passionate nature, a kind of devilish nature, are lovingly searching for a human person, or a situation, against which they can knock their heads, and they despise any partner or situation in which their passion wins out. Instinctively they seek defeat. It is as if something within them knows this devil has to be hit on the head, which is why if one is friendly or weak, or understanding towards such fire, one does not help the person; generally such people walk out on you, because that is not what they want. The fire of the passion looks for that which will extinguish it, and that is why the urge for individuation, as long as it is a natural inordinate urge, seeks impossible situations; it seeks conflict and defeat and suffering because it seeks its own transformation.* [From *Alchemy: An Introduction to the Symbolism and the Psychology*]

If I could get the better of you in a debate about the nature of reality, say, I'd probably find it hard to sustain the level of respect for you I've always had. I suppose that's one aspect of what I've meant by the creative tension of the opposites, and as Jung stressed, a state of conflict indicates closeness to God. Far from being perversely idealistic, this sort of binary star-like 'duelism' is — at least to my way of seeing things — necessary if a particular kind of psychic growth is to occur. Perhaps, though, the whole thing's more like a less drastic version of the koan-ish impasse of the irresistible force meeting the immovable object. The other side of it is that, for my part at least, friendliness and understanding have never been weak, forced, placatory, or compromising responses to you. It's simply that I'm far too fond of you to react differently; plus my instinct, as you know, has always been to seek the resolving synthesis. But does any of this make sense, or am I merely being excessively scrutinising?

To be honest, I've often felt frustrated yet strangely relieved that I've never been able to get the upper hand. Neither, in my honest estimation, have you. Perhaps this relates to my most commonly recurring dream, in which I'm prevented from flying too high by threatening and sentient 'power lines' that suddenly appear across the sky. The dreams also reveal a kind of Icarus complex, a tendency toward imaginal escapism which is thwarted at every turn. They could also be an instance of my 'power devil' (von Franz's term) being thwarted from its tendency toward hubris. Since I've known you, this dream, which for almost ten years I'd had on average once a fortnight, has almost totally ceased, so I'm led to suspect that you've helped me exorcise this particular demon. I've recently had some very 'positive' dreams about you, by the way, in which you were finally free from the damaging influences of your past.

I truly admire your prolific writerly output, particularly since my own pattern of creativity normally consists of sporadic bursts of activity interpolated with lengthier, though never unproductive bouts of lethargy, too often conveniently rationalised as necessary phases of gestative inspiration. Nonetheless, major revelations have been gently dropping like snowflake mandalas into the soul; no, not turning thence, I assure you, to water on the brain. Speaking of watery allusions (and fluid concepts), your comment a couple of letters ago about the 'foetid swamps' of alchemy drew a smile from me, not out of condescension or as a result of Buddha-like detachment, but because I've come to recognise that 'this also is thou; neither is this thou'. In fact, at the time I'd just finished reading a book called *Jung and Astrology* — much of which I disagreed with — in which Jung and Freud's relationship was discussed at length. Overall, theirs was a classic instance of the thinking extravert (Freud) humbugging the intuitive introvert (Jung). Perhaps in a way you've had for some time a Freud and a Jung battling within you(?).

An intriguing incident between them occurred when Freud asked Jung to promise that he would never abandon the sexual theory, because Freud wished it to remain a dogma, an 'unshakable bulwark'. Jung later recalled: 'In some astonishment I asked him, "A bulwark – against what?" To which [Freud] replied, "Against the black tide of mud" [cf. your "foetid swamps"] and here he hesitated for a moment, then added – "of occultism"'. Yet Freud's attitude to occultism remained ambivalent as he oscillated repeatedly between scepticism and credulity. Eventually his curiosity led to his becoming a member of the Society of Psychical Research, which led to his uncovering in analysis instances of telepathy, thence to attempt to align psychoanalysis with psychical research. At the same time, he never lost a questioning and rational attitude, such that their exchange was primarily a contrast of temperament and typology, rather than a lack of critical ability and honesty on either part. I can see some of Freud's conflict in you, particularly in view of the extent to which alchemy, myth, goddesses, mystical symbols and religion feature in your own works, and in light of your sporadic awareness of ways in which archetypes have been active in shaping and energising your own life journey.

Reflecting on our past exchanges, your zealous antagonism to matters holistic has at times reminded me in principle of St Paul (and C. S. Lewis, come to think of it), both of whose fervent hatred of Christianity reverted to its opposite. I hope it goes without saying that this is meant as a compliment in that this kind of *enantiodromia* only happens to souls of immense potential, who can never espouse mediocrity but because of their passion for life, or enormous energy gradient, or however one describes it, can embrace only extremes of one kind or another. In this sense you're by far the most passionate man I've ever known, but then I'm no less passionate a woman.

So of course I understand that you've needed to vent your annoyance, frustration and conflict on me, partly, as perhaps you'll concede, because I personify that with which you're at war, inwardly as well as outwardly. Whatever the reason — for I don't intend to insult you by trying to analyse the situation further — I'm not and never have been your enemy, as well you know. Sure, I don't always agree with you, but then neither would I ever reject you, or stop encouraging and supporting you, or belittle your integrity, or try to hurt you in any way. Whether you can accept it or not, you're deeply cared for and no amount of complaining about foetid swamps, or other dismal liquids will make it otherwise. Besides, I've never doubted, even when you've been at your angriest, that behind your touchy exterior hides a gentle and sensitive man. And regardless of how intellectually astute and successful a writer you might be, if I didn't know those subdued qualities to be just as real, I couldn't care for you and think as highly of you as I do.

I'd still like to listen to that alchemy tape of yours, so am pestering you again with a request to send it over. Goodness, just because it's about alchemy doesn't mean I automatically assumed it would be a sane and balanced treatment of the subject. You know I'm no more open to (what you call) 'mental self-pollution' (aha — water again!) than you are. After all, I can no more deny what I've experienced as real than I could deny my own existence. I know (as intuited *gnosis*), therefore I am. Who knows, I might have judged the tape to be a load of codswallop. In fact I probably would have if, as you mentioned, it's about literally making manna. I was simply curious to see how the guy's ideas compared with those of Jung and von Franz.

This year I'm down to teach a Uni of SA subject drearily titled 'Technical Communication'. It's a compulsory course in literacy skills which all faculties, including Civil Aviation, Computing, Journalism and Chemical Engineering have to include, so I'll possibly end up with an unimaginative bunch of students. I've also divided — at the suggestion of the Uni of Adelaide — my sf course into two separate courses, one called 'Science Fiction, Psyche and Science' and the other, by request, solely on Jungian dream analysis. I've been receiving a steady stream of 'patients' for therapy, though not enough to earn a living from, so it's just as well that I've got the teaching jobs to fall back on.

On the reading front, I loved *Green Mars* and am now scouting about for *Blue*. What particularly impressed me was Robinson's ability to evoke the sense of what I'd call the 'technological sublime'. (Have you come across anyone else using that term?) The sheer scope and grandeur of some of his Martian technology educes a kind of mystical reverence and awe, for instance a scene which wonderfully describes the ten metre thick collapsed space-elevator draped across a large crater basin into the airless distance.

I've saved all your letters, by the way, even the nasty ones, plus most of my replies. Hey, maybe we could edit and publish them anonymously in book form some day. Perhaps we could call it *Letters To and from a Skiffy Scribbler and a Black Holist.*

25 April 1996

Dear Damien

I hope you had a pleasant birthday celebration and that the anticipated dinner invite from friends materialised?

I'm truly sorry, though somewhat startled, to hear about the Atheling ballot result, given the amount of thought, time and care you put into *Reading by Starlight,* and the apparent meagreness of the winning effort, which I haven't read. Still, the verdict doesn't detract from the excellence of your own work but perhaps reflects, as you've suggested it might, the bias of Perth fandom. I suppose you can take some comfort, though, in A's exuberant response to *White Abacus,* and in that US guy's desire to quote your e-interview in his next book. What's happening with your collaborative version of Schrödinger's Dog? Have Deakin UP decided yet whether they want to publish your *Theory* book?

In response to my own applications to US publishers, I've received 12 rejections and am still waiting on the big ones: Princeton, Cambridge and Oxford. Meanwhile, Mellen have started sending impatient, even faintly sarcastic notes wondering why I haven't yet sent them the manuscript, so I'm trying to stall and appease them for a while longer.

Interesting that in response to my New Age letter, you homed in on a part I weeded out for publication. In response to your query, though, the '12 years of training' I mentioned included everything — including many hours of paid-for, private analysis — that in Jung's view fits under this heading. However, because the analysis I underwent wasn't under the auspices of ANZSJA (which didn't exist then anyway), it wasn't recorded as training, but other than that there was no difference in what was involved. Hence I appreciate your ongoing reservations, and while to some degree I've shared them, on a deeper, more intuitive level I no longer do. What I didn't mention in the New Age letter is that Jung allows for an alternative to a training analysis, namely the possibility of analysing oneself through one's patients, which works only if one has an uncompromising passion for 'truth at all costs'. Of course, the irony attached to the desirability of a training analysis is that Jung himself never underwent one, but was obliged to fall back on his own intuitions, experiences and gropings in the dark. I, solely for financial reasons, have had to opt for a similar route, given the exorbitant cost of private sessions with an analyst.

Thus out of financial necessity rather than choice I haven't completely towed the line as far as professional credentials and 'respectability' go, but does my character count for so little that you're prepared to side with a cultural bias and socioeconomic guideline? Come on Damien, I know you to be a fine judge of character, so judge me according to whatever integrity you've perceived in me. And stop pretending to be totally objective about it all when you know as well as I do that there's more to your uneasiness than concerns over 'qualifications'.

Not long after my critical phase of 'borderline psychosis' (1983–4), I decided I wanted to be an analyst. The decision came from the ego and was promptly quashed when I met Jung in a dream and was 'advised' by him to forget it and instead concentrate on getting to know myself. In the dream, we were walking together across a meadow in bright moonlight. Another figure was coming toward us from the far side. As it drew nearer, I recognised the figure to be me. She came close and stood facing me wordlessly. Jung then said to me, with a hint of sarcasm, 'Now you're ready to talk with someone'. End of dream. I took his advice.

My studies much further down the track of Keats, alchemy, shamanism, and other esoteric fields, were the result of years of wrestling with the unconscious and trying to make sense of it all. Ditto template for Jung, who always confessed that his early eruptions from the unconscious formed the basis of all his later work. The upshot is that therapy is now no longer what I merely want to do; it's what I must do, and although I understand your misgivings I have no choice but to heed the call. The reality is that I could no more resist it than a serpent can resist shedding her skin. Nonetheless, I continue to discuss the kinds of reservations you have with other 'Jungians' and have in the meantime undergone as much analysis as I can afford.

As I confessed in the New Age letter, 'I've only just begun to learn'; nor do I have the gall to call myself an 'analyst', a label which only folk who've studied through one of the Jung Institutes are entitled to, but only ever refer to myself as a 'therapist'. The counterbalance is that I'm the only person in Adelaide who's done an original PhD in the Jungian field, which surely counts for something. The other 'therapists' have done mainstream psychology degrees in which, as they lament, Jung wasn't even mentioned. At least Jungians recognise the need for the analysis of the analyst, in whatever context it occurs. Psychiatrists and mainstream psychologists generally don't and so often end up floundering in the dark, or projecting their neuroses, latent psychoses, or shadows onto patients.

But the issue of 'paying for analysis' is one that Jungians are still grappling with, and one London Institute is currently setting up an alternative training scheme where non-financial trainees 'pay' through work exchange. I've been discussing all this with a Jungian analyst. As she confessed to me, she was lucky in that her husband forked out for her to train for 5 years in London while he had a job there. The other side of this coin is that Jung, Christ, Buddha and Mother Teresa (for examples) never did a training analysis, not that I'd ever be arrogant enough to compare myself to souls of their calibre, but the principle holds true: they responded first and foremost to a calling to the healing vocation. After all, I doubt whether any of the latter three would have been able to afford analysis either.

Of course there are two equally valid sides to the issue; I see that as clearly as anyone, which is precisely why I penned that New Age letter, but I've simply chosen the only option open to me at this time. It's not as though I've done nothing in the Jungian field, whereas this is the case with the 'spiritual healer' I was having a go at in the New Age letter, a 'clairvoyant' whom I know has no Jungian qualifications of any kind and who has, since the publication of my letter, stopped advertising herself as a 'counsellor' offering 'Jungian analysis', so I must have hit the nail on the head.

Speaking of 'dodgy' credentials, I've recently come across several sensitive and bewildered folk who've been harmed — in one instance to the point of attempted suicide — by psychiatrists who've refused to take what was happening to them (including dreams or visions) seriously, or who have handed them drugs and told them to snap out of it, or pull themselves together. Kindness, respect and an empathic ear cost little to offer, but it seems that even $200 an hour can't buy such gifts from some 'professionals'. All this aside, analysis work is demanding and sometimes exhausting. Like your brand of writing, it can be lonely, and it earns little in the way of public appreciation, or financial reward. But I could no more stop trying to help others find their true path than you could cease writing. You write because you must, because it's an expression of the urge to life within you, which is what makes you a true writer. I do my best in my field because I must. In the end it comes down to this heart-centred imperative.

Anyway, this is getting morbidly labyrinthine and introspective and you're no doubt sick and tired of hearing about Jungian matters. The truth is, though, I've probably done more self-analysis through knowing you than through any other relationship. After all is said and done, I still believe that you and I could learn a great deal more from one another, but it's becoming harder to do so now that you've emotionally armoured yourself to the almost impenetrable extent that you have. I love you, but I know that this could never mean anything to you until you're prepared to stop hating yourself and allow yourself to be loved, and unless you could acknowledge that perhaps you need me as much as I need and stand to learn from you.

The Mythopoeic folk are still convening, at a different venue and with a new committee. I'm no longer a member but turn up to meetings of potential interest, such as T's new round of talks on Blake last Friday. I disagreed (as usual) with his interpretation of key Blake texts, which livened up the evening considerably. Basically, I think his Christian background blinds him to the realisation that Blake's 'system' transcends religious moralism and orthodox Christianity. Still, the meetings are usually stimulating and socially enjoyable. Next month we'll be discussing mythic elements in various sf films, including *The Incredible Shrinking Man.*

The other night I had a dream about Paul Davies. We were both involved in a canoeing venture, during which he ticked me off for calling him 'Paul' instead of 'Prof. Davies'. I later wondered if perhaps this was a rebuking compensation for the presumptuously chummy tone of my letter to him. A few days later my suspicion was confirmed when I received a reply from his secretary, thanking me on Paul's behalf for the von Franz material I sent him, and regretting that on account of his hectic schedule he wouldn't have time to answer my theoretical questions.

Given your recent chilly tone, I was somewhat taken aback to receive your note plus the gift of the Allaby book last month. Thank you for the kind thought, though, since I've enjoyed the read and found his historical and cultural overview to be particular lively and well-informed. As to why I've been hesitant, even undecided about responding, I trust you can appreciate that being repeatedly, even if 'only' verbally beaten by you has been emotionally exhausting and ultimately demoralising, as well as simply too painful to endure any further. As I've said, although I understand why you've needed to react the way you have, I feel that things moved some time ago beyond the point where my allowing you to keep hurting and ridiculing me would benefit either of us.

I was confused by your former confession that you'd rather be lonely than put up with my mystical quirks, and your later decision that you wanted to keep the lines of communication open between us. So I need to know whether at least a part of you can still enjoy, or be challenged, or even possibly enriched by our continued communication. Please don't evade the question, Dayananda. You're an excellent communicator, better than me when you choose to be. And regardless of how much you distance, armour, or disguise your true self, I can only ever be open and personal toward you, since to be otherwise would be to deny my deepest nature and feelings.

I took your gift, then, as some sort of conciliatory gesture, which suggests an uncertainty of attitude on your part toward me. I still have a wonderful long letter you wrote in May '95 in which you opened up and explored the possible motivations for your conflict, which included your sense of weak boundaries and the need to over-defend against anything that was a sublimation of your former 'spiritual' foe, Catholicism. I'm wondering whether you've had any more insights about this, but I don't want to press the issue.

Getting back to Allaby — of course I didn't sympathise with his critique of holism. Craftily smuggling 'science' into the book's subtitle, he aims to hoodwink undiscerning readers into believing that instead of defending a psychological bias, he's putting forward 'the case for science', a phrase implying that 'science' and 'reductionism' are interchangeable terms. The holists, of course, are no less presumptuous, as is evident in a Wilber subtitle: 'Exploring the leading edge of science'. Neither party will come clean and admit that since science is about the way we perceive and interpret reality, rather than about reality as it is, individual as well as cultural subjective biases are inherent in all scientific discourse. Hence, and as I've tried to discuss with you before, holists are usually intuitives (and often introverts), while reductionists are predominantly extraverted thinking types. The upshot is that the debate will remain circular on both sides as long as each party assumes its own perspective to be normal, more scientific, more intelligent, or less biased than its opposite.

Allaby's accusations of holists as being childish, sentimental, naive or fearful thus tell me more about his personal psychology, in particular his religious, intuitive shadow, than they do about science. 'I am interested in many things outside myself', says he as a typical extravert, hence in contrast with introverts he naturally finds 'deep introspection boring and unproductive' (p. 30). Introverts, on the other hand, would say something like: 'I'm interested in many things inside myself and find the focus on outer facts boring and unproductive'. Dear oh dear. There's room enough on this planet, not to mention between you and me, for both perspectives, surely. I'd like to respond in much greater detail to the book, but I'm not sure whether you're still open to the possibility, even desirability of our learning from one another.

You mentioned that a 'couple of books hang by threads'. What news on that front? Are your *Theory* and *Transrealism* books still in the running for publication? I enjoyed reading *Science Fiction* #36. Russell's article, in particular, I found zestful, insightful and subtly affectionate. He captured your complexity, depth and ambivalence brilliantly — 'vaguely demonic' versus 'gnostic saint' indeed. I couldn't have put it better myself. I'm also thrilled on your and Rory's behalf to hear that HarperCollins have accepted *Zones* for next year. Congrats to you both!

I've just finished Robert Holdstock's *Where Time Winds Blow,* lovely, eerie stuff with a neat twist at the end, when it's revealed that what was assumed to be a time displacement that's dumping alien artefacts from past and future into a present valley, is really a wind-like life-form solidifying its dreams and desires. I've also just finished a book by yer ol' mate Robert Johnson on the omnipotent wiles of the mother complex — against which even Sophia is powerless — and another, comparing Reich and Jung, on the body as shadow.

Aside from teaching and marking illiterate assignments at the Uni of SA, a few months back I scored a weekly radio program called 'Jung at Heart'. Our signature tune is the old Sinatra version of 'Young at Heart', which contains some apt lyrics: 'You can go to extremes with impossible schemes/ You can laugh when your dreams fall apart at the seams'. The show is a deft blend of news, music and discussions of UFO encounters, plus dream and art material sent in by post. No effort is made to interpret dreams, since to do so without consulting the dreamer would violate the ethics of Jungian analysis. Currently I'm toying with the idea of livening up the show by penning some 5 minute scripts for a serial, 'Jung in Space', in which intrepid space explorers encounter black clouds, singularities, shadowy aliens. and other metaphors for the psyche's anatomy. I've also been offered a spot on a Channel 7 AM program which deals with alternative approaches to mainstream medicine. Last week I did an ABC talkback segment during which people phoned in to ask about their 'weird' dreams. It worked so well that they've invited me back for more.

I'm glad to hear you're having so much fun on the net. Did you catch a recent segment on ABC's 'Compass' in which they reviewed some ludicrous new Catholic confessional websites? In response to the computer screen's opening question, 'What is thy sin, my child?' one is required to click one of the Seven Deadlies to get the ball rolling.

What do you think of the *Trek* 'Voyager' series? What's annoying about their unimaginative indoor alien sets is that they're always dotted about with large pot plants, seemingly always of the same species, regardless of which planet they're on. Still, on the whole the script standard is high and I'm guessing that the holographic doctor, along the same lines as Data, has the greatest potential for character development.

I don't know about e-mail being preferable to snailmail, if speed is the sole advantage of the latter. Anyway, being, as you know I am, a Taoist, I'm seldom in a hurry but prefer instead a more gestative and fermentative approach, a residence in *kairos* rather than Kronos time, a sense of life flowing irresistibly toward its goal, like the root which without pause or haste makes its way around all obstacles.

Take care, Dayananda.

6 May 1996

Dear Damien

There's not a lot I can, or need say in response to your last letter. Strange that 'me simply being me' has come to cause you such annoyance, frustration and anger, while I've continued to value your personal uniqueness. But I'm not one to go where I'm not wanted, nor is it in my nature to be 'intrusive' or demanding in any way, since I'd never tolerate the same from anyone else. So of course your words were hurtful, but I sense that this time you've wounded yourself more, and in a vastly different way, than you've hurt me.

I have no desire to be regarded as a source of 'harassment', since nothing could ever be further from my life's overall intent. My friendship is always freely, but never lightly or indiscriminately offered, as a gift, not as a burden to be grudgingly borne. If it's not wanted and brings neither enjoyment nor enrichment to another, then it quietly returns to itself, gains new calm and strength, and goes where it is valued elsewhere. If, as you've accepted, I've only ever shown you 'kindness' and 'well-wishing', then how can you suggest that my love for you is not genuine? Are not kindness and well-wishing facets of genuine love?

Since I first dreamed of you as burnt and crippled, I vaguely hoped, I suppose, that if I allowed you to wound me it might somehow help heal your own wounds. Making and maintaining this choice have cost me more than you can ever know, and I freely admit that I have failed, but I don't regret the choice, since I've learnt a great deal from it and have at least meant to do you good. So yes, you have indeed wounded me — which isn't the same thing as peevishly 'being hurt' — and yes, I trust that it has helped you in some way.

There's a finer line than you might suppose between gladly taking up the yoke of a 'Wounded Healer' and masochism, but

I feel that to continue with the way things have become would be, for me at least, stepping over that line into something that could become damaging, instead of being a spur to advance my and your growth. So although your respect has always meant a great deal to me, I'm not prepared to forego my own self-respect and integrity in order to keep it. As long as I believed there was no genuine dislike on your part toward me — that, in other words, your anger and frustration were really being directed elsewhere — I felt that this 'voluntary wounding' might have been helping you resolve certain painful issues from your past. But since, as it now seems, I've lost whatever affection you once had for me, there remain no grounds, surely, on which to continue our communication.

You knew from the start where I was coming from, in terms of where life had already guided me. As the mystic you perhaps needed to remind you of the spiritual realities you've spurned, I did not seem so repulsive to you then. You even thought that I'd be 'just the person' to write a book about your work, even though you knew from what angle I'd be writing it. I've never tried to hide my intuitions and spiritual experiences, however bizarre they might seem, from you, nor at one stage did you wish me to do so. But whereas over time my fondness for you has grown, for some reason the inverse seems to have happened for you.

I'm sorry to hear that you no longer enjoy *Trek.* For all its inane moralising and stupidities, it still has some enjoyably healthy escapism and harmless laughs to offer. But what's happened to you, Dayananda? It's not so long ago that you seemed to be more open to savouring the flawed fun of such offerings. You'll hate me saying this, but more and more you've come to remind me of Jonas Cord in *The Carpetbaggers,* a crass book, I know, but his father-derived self-hatred is relevant in your case. I hope, though, for the sake of your potential happiness, that in time you'll come to the same kind of liberating realisation that in the end both 'defeated' and rescued him.

To me the saddest thing of all is that you choose to believe that the love I've offered you is a 'fantasy', instead of accepting that you're a lovable and worthwhile human being, for in doing so you give the victory to one of Catholicism's greatest lies, hence the lie to me. But I won't take up any more of your time, now or in the future. I shall take the opportunity, though, to wish you your deepest good and happiness, whatever, wherever, and whoever that may be.

Science Fiction Conference Paper

Myths of Inner and Outer Space: Science Fiction and the Quest for Transcendence

by Maureen B. Roberts BSc, PhD

Presented at the 11th International Conference of the Mythopoeic Literature Society of Australia [July 1994]

To quote from J. G. Ballard: 'By day fantastic birds flew through the petrified forests, and jewelled alligators glittered like heraldic salamanders on the banks of the crystalline rivers. By night the illuminated man raced among the trees, his arms like golden cartwheels, his head like a spectral crown'. It sounds like the stuff of myth and fantasy, yet this is a work of science fiction by an author who with a Conrad-like, almost suffocating density of image and symbolic meaning evokes in his novel *The Crystal World* the metaphysical landscapes of soul, through a Daliesque dwarfing of the individual by the immense energies of the unconscious as they are echoed in Nature. Set in a West African jungle, an apocalyptic crystallisation of the universe into living gems unfolds, when through a time contraction all is 'transfigured and illuminated, joined together in the last marriage of time and space'. Matter and anti-matter, time and anti-time are mutually annihilated into timelessness.

If Ballard's vision is the ironic nemesis of Nature too long abused through the hubris of technocracy, it nonetheless anticipates the transcendence of dualism in all its guises. However bizarre the apotheosis, it involves the surrender of a lone self to an existence unbound by spatial and temporal restrictions, a self whose fate mirrors the fate of the universe to which he is inextricably tied. Since the 1960s, much of science fiction as prophetic mythology has anticipated key changes that are emerging into our collective awareness. As a reflection of radical shifts in the meanings of 'science' and 'God', our age is witnessing a dramatic upheaval of consciousness, through a humanisation of the universe and a corresponding deification of humanity. This trend reflects our quest for selfhood as completeness — as a relatedness that seeks to unite the many polarities of life — dark and light, male and female, inner and outer, Nature and technology, human and divine, science and mythology.

In science fiction, along with the stock motifs of parallel universes and time travel, we find metaphysics, utopianism, shape-shifting, gender-swapping, cybernetics, psionics, God; anything is fair game in this genre's role as mediator between science and imagination in our quest to transcend the limitations of mundane existence. But this escapism is neither (to paraphrase Tolkien) the flight of the deserter nor the legitimate escape of the prisoner. It is, rather, the search for a new paradigm of reality which reflects our collective evolution of consciousness.

Myth is both a response to the emerging needs of a culture and an impetus for its change. As a dramatisation of archetypal patterns and themes, myth is a mirror held up to the collective soul. Myth-makers are prophetic voices who transpose the universal themes of myth into a contemporary setting, in order to deal with questions triggered by the deplorable state of the world and the sense of meaninglessness in a materialistic society. Science fiction both questions and sanctions the directions society takes, because its response to scientific progress is ambivalent.

Science fiction can warn us of the dangers of inflation, arrogance, hubris and nemesis. The 1950s, for instance, got stuck in a conflict between science and Nature through a deification of deterministic science and the backlash of a mass neurosis over Nature. Humans armed with technology triggered Nature's revenge, as the dragons and monsters of traditional mythology became a giantism of natural imagery: a fly, rabbits, ants, walking plants, dinosaurs, The Giant Claw, The Spider, The Blob, the Creature From the Black Lagoon, all angry symbols of the rejected instinctive realm. This was a time when mechanistic science, idealistically fuelled with high-powered futurism and the illusion of omnipotence, saved the day.

Since then the inflated notion of science as conquest has been superseded by the theme of a humble search for harmony with Nature and alien cultures, a quest championed by authors such as Ray Bradbury, Ursula Le Guin, Larry Niven, C. J. Cherryh, Gregory Benford, David Brin, Walter Miller, and others. Can myth and technological progress coexist? Indeed it can. Science fiction transposes technology into the context of contemporary myth, a challenge from which fantasy, in spite of it being usually healthy escapism, makes a sometimes cowardly retreat. If fantasy's defect is its exclusiveness, that is, its omission of technology, science fiction's merit is its inclusive ability to absorb every facet of modern culture into a mythic vision.

At the heart of myth is the archetypal essence of human nature, the transcendental centre and circumferential whole of the Jungian 'self', which is coextensive with the cosmos and experientially indistinguishable from God. If myth is inclusive by virtue of its holism, so then is its unifying core self, which transcends the polarities of matter and psyche, inner and outer, Nature and technology. Hence in Vernor Vinge's *A Fire Upon the Deep*, the mythologising of computer networking unfolds on a cosmic scale through a heroic struggle against a technopsychic 'Perversion', which is threatening to destabilise the galactic 'Known Net' and its Zone borders. In Vinge's scheme, different planetary races explore paths to a 'Transcendence' whose supremacy is hazily defined in terms of technological superiority. Vinge's division of the mandala-like galaxy into 'Zones of Thought' mirrors the hierarchical structure of the psyche, moving outward from the 'The Unthinking Depths' of the unconscious Core, through the

Great Slowness, to the Beyond, and finally to the outermost 'Transcend' where godlike 'Powers' dwell.

There is perhaps a similar mythic intent in Damien Broderick's *The Dreaming Dragons*, which portrays a symbolic reality in which a 'transcendent computer' induces a godlike consciousness through which machines, a centaur, angelic archetypes and the aboriginal Serpent Dreaming coexist in a 'universe of discourse' where inner and outer reality merge into one consciousness, one technomythic existence. At the culmination of the novel, earthly wisdom is revealed as culminating in 'spirit and matter brought together in life knowing itself', when the questing protagonists move inward through ten spheres of progressive enlightenment toward the central singularity of ultimate truth. In *The Dreaming Dragons* Broderick presents an intriguing rationale for the Platonic idea of the World Soul, or the collective unconscious, which originates as a constructed 'Soul Core', a spherical locus of wisdom located in a Central Australian 'Vault' made by ancestral prehuman saurians.

In these novels we witness the trend to literalise the symbolic, to merge gods and humans through the erosion of a clear distinction between fact and myth. Such visions perhaps foresee that technology and consciousness may eventually fuse into an alchemical synthesis transcending both material and immaterial existence. Through an evolutionary imperative, humanity gropes from one paradigm of reality to another; by exploring existential questions of identity and apocalyptic visions of transformation, science fiction dramatises the fragmentedness, complexity and mystery of who we are. To quote the motto of Star Trek's 'Deep Space Nine' series: 'It is the unknown that defines our existence'. The relativity of mass, space and time echoes the kaleidoscopic shuffling and reformation of our identity. But paradoxically a kaleidoscope image is ordered, for in the self, as in the cosmos, harmony and dissolution into chaos coexist in creative tension.

As Kim Stanley Robinson suggests, successive scientific eras zig-zag between alternating paradigms of reality, from the illusory stability of determinism to the fluid boundaries of relativity. The oscillation between integration and disintegration mirrors the cyclic dance of the psyche. In science fiction the search for identity involves fundamental questions about knowledge, and the nature and scope of the psyche, as we midwife a new consciousness in which there are as many universes as there are souls to experience them. In this regard the quasi-mystical view of science has fostered the burgeoning of science fiction's metaphysical dimension.

In the new, holistic paradigm of science the theoretical emphasis is no longer on detached analysis, but rather on interaction, complementarity, synchronicity, and relatedness, reflecting the supposition that energy, matter and consciousness share an unknown common ground. In describing the universe as a great idea, though, we are not implying the existence of an overarching deity but are rather suggesting that psyche *per se* pervades the universe. Philip K. Dick embraces the pre-Socratic view that the 'cosmos is not as it appears to be, and what it probably is, at its deepest level, is exactly what the human being is at his [or her] deepest level — call it mind or soul, it is something unitary which lives and thinks, and only appears to be plural and material.... The universe, then, is thinker and thought, and since we are part of it, we as humans are, in the final analysis, thoughts of and thinkers of those thoughts'.

In microphysics an observer is postulated in objective reality. In our age of relativity, uncertainty as the prime ingredient of quantum theory leads us to conclude that the reality which the observation sharpens into focus cannot be separated from the observer. Reality, then, is not empirical; the universe achieves a knowable existence only as a result of our perception of it. It is in some sense created by its own inhabitants. The allied theory of parallel universes might well give rise to cosmic schizophrenia, for if the unity of psyche and cosmos postulated by Jung and theoretical physicists implies on one level the coincidence of subjectivity and universal truth, the other side of the coin is that it gives rise to a personal crisis of knowledge, perception and existence. In this regard, Dick, perhaps better than any other science fiction writer, manages to integrate both sides of the challenge and dilemma.

As metafictions of the spirit-matter dualism of Gnosticism, many of Dick's metaphors of individual alienation can also be read as allegories of the ignorance which binds us to a fake reality, and blinds us to the 'gnosis', or heart-centred certainty of our true, eternal identity. Hence although Dick's spirit-matter dualism is at odds with the emerging holism of our age, VALIS, his cosmic 'Vast Active Living Information System', is envisioned in *Radio Free Albemuth* as a 'great universe of transmitting and receiving stations', like brain synapses.

If the universe is more like a great idea than a great machine, for those who value intimacy there's comfort to be gained from this more personal paradigm. The shift of perspective undermines the 'Logos' of verbal discrimination by 'Eros', the feminine principle of empathy and relatedness that understands through acquaintance and participation, such that detachment is no longer even a respectable theoretical option. In Dan Simmons' *The Fall of Hyperion* amidst high-tech gateways and networks, AI's threaten to build a 'God of Machines', a technology void of relatedness. Understandably, it is the unborn female child of emerging human consciousness who is to counteract — through becoming 'the One Who Teaches' — the knowledge needed for the 'junction of human spirit and AI logic'.

In exploring our parameters of knowledge and existence, science fiction is able to depict the godlike role of human consciousness in shaping reality and codetermining the very fabric of the universe. Greg Egan incorporates the conscious manipulation of quantum probability states in *Quarantine*, while in Le Guin's earlier *The Lathe of Heaven* we witness the awesome power and frightening predicament of a man who repeatedly wakens from his changing dreams of the world, only to find the world to be as he has dreamed it.

Although this PhilDickian brand of cognitive dissonance shatters one reality construct after another, it is as well an indictment of the omnipotence of mind. That aside, Dick's two main recurrent questions: 'What is real?' and 'What does it mean to be human?' remain at the fore of science fiction's explorations of inner and outer space. As with Arthur C. Clarke's brand of transcendental evolution, if through alien intervention we are passive recipients of a preordained cosmic destiny, as human gods we are not merely pawns, or sub-creators but rather makers of our own reality. Thus in Dan Simmons' *The Hollow Man* the mind of a dying, retarded boy becomes a new universe for a man and his dead wife; her resurrection is not the gift of an all-powerful God, but rather is bestowed, ironically, by the most helpless of human beings.

Simmons also raises quasi-mystical notions about the collapsing of quantum probability structures, as his protagonist announces that 'without us, the universe would be pure duality, infinite probability sets', that is, chaotic, whereas through us the universe condenses out from a blur of possibilities into a focused, finite reality. This is the stuff of philosophical intrigue. Did Relativity exist before Einstein's theories of it? Such questions border on the mystical, yet in Simmons' words it is 'without the absurdities of religion' that we can respond to 'the spiritual potential of the universe', by allowing it to collapse into any one of its countless possibilities.

Here we find a coincidence of idea and reality in the form of a special mode of existence. Can we perhaps say, then, that what we envision in space are the outer occasions for an inner dialectical journey? As Brian Aldiss, commenting on Greg Bear's *Blood Music* succinctly puts it: 'Inner space is our evolutionary future'. From within this synchronistic paradigm, black holes could not have been discovered until their theoretical foundations had been established; as Einstein says: 'It is the theory which decides what we can observe'.

As our significance in the universe becomes godlike, we realise that the boundless energies of the cosmos are also within us. Psychically, the unconscious is a relative space-time continuum. Black holes and neutron stars on one hand symbolise the threat of nonexistence and on the other, the extreme pressure of existence that we feel. The science in science fiction is not a replacement for older mythologies, rather, as Ursula Le Guin comments, 'its originality is that it uses the myth-making faculty on new material'. The archetypal God-image of centre and circumference becomes the invisible inner point, the singularity surrounded by its spherical black hole whose outer event horizon mirrors the interface between conscious and unconscious. Through exploiting the creative and destructive potential of this cosmic phenomenon, the central singularity mirrors the transcendent core of our being as a region where all rules fail. And if paradoxically this is a form of certainty, like us, the universe is also illogical and shadowy, incomplete and fragmented.

Kim Stanley Robinson's *The Memory of Whiteness* concerns the melding of a new form of deterministic physics with music and philosophy, whereby 'the Music of the Spheres' is given new meaning. In this futuristic vision, by contracting solar energy to singularities within spherical discontinuities, hundreds of asteroids and moons of our solar system are colonised as self-sustaining orbs. Using a mythic structure, the tale involves a questing journey for ultimate truth, undertaken by a physicist/musician from outer to inner space, from a peripheral vision on Pluto to the insight gained in the glaring, solar light at the centre. In the end the travelling cosmic Orchestra and its leader spin toward the singularity point of a cone and are destroyed, symbolising, perhaps, the abolition of conscious belief as it submits to the higher wisdom of the transcendent self.

In Greg Bear's 'The Venging' a scientific expedition to a black hole is subsumed by mythic and religious themes involving the ship's voyage into darkness, transformation, self-confrontation, and a transcendent peace experienced by the travellers, culminating in an ironic descent into the hell of a stagnant parallel universe. With equal irony, for an allied, more primitive, alien culture the same black hole is a place of ritualistic burial from which haunting music intermittently returns.

The gods of myth personify ruling archetypal ideas which are morally ambivalent and so have dark and light faces. Responding to the expansion of our social horizons into the cosmos, the gods became the aliens who also have 'good' and 'bad' faces as either our saviours, or invaders. Our views of aliens are projections of our own hopes, fears and anxieties, often as unconscious responses to where we feel 'progressive' scientific trends might sometimes be leading us. More highly evolved aliens can be indistinguishable from God, or gods, as in *2001*, where an apparently benevolent Overmind guides us in our destiny to attain a godlike transcendence of spacetime corporality. The familiar mythic themes appear: symbolic death leading to rebirth as the Divine Child, the descent into the unknown, the isolation of the lone quester, the 4-fold Monolith as the technomystical symbol of unity and transformation.

Clarke's earlier *Childhood's End* concerns our expulsion from innocence into a godlike state of existence, by aliens who appear indistinguishable from devils. The evolved humans are finally able to dream their way out into space, by melting the interface between inner and outer, while through the paradox of the 'fortunate fall' into godlike knowledge, evil is seen as an artificial human construct, formulated in response to our fear of transformation into a more highly evolved state.

In Philip José Farmer's *Maker of Universes*, godlike, world-creating cosmic kidnappers are metaphorically revealed to be tyrannical aspects of ourselves — ambivalent archetypal forces which we must confront and channel in positive ways. Pride reverts to humility when the main character, Wolff, discovers that he, as a former hedonistic planet-maker, has been reincarnated on Earth. Eventually he confronts his previous cruelty and ruthlessness and returns to rule as an enlightened being. And in Farmer's later *To Your Scattered Bodies Go*, unseen, godlike beings resurrect everyone who has ever lived along the banks of a huge, alien river.

Inverting this perspective, it is we, rather than an advanced alien culture, who become the gods whom beings of other worlds strive to emulate. Mythologically, if the aliens are indistinguishable from gods, they are ultimately indistinguishable from us. Such is the message of Robert Silverberg's *Kingdoms of the Wall*, which depicts the ritual ascent of a chosen group of alien pilgrims to the summit of a mountain on which strange gods — in reality astronauts from Earth — have appeared throughout the ages. Since the time of the Christlike 'First Climber' the pilgrims have been taught that this summit 'is a place where the power of the gods is so great that change comes freely and amazingly to those who live their lives upon it, and all is magic and mystery and strangeness beyond [their] comprehension'. One character muses that those 'who live in Heaven are gods', since their 'homes are the stars, and the stars are fire. Who can live in fire except a god?'

Our responsibility — inferred from Jung's revolutionary *Answer to Job* — is to continue the realisation of the divine self which occurs through self-knowledge, a theme hinted at with uncanny foresight in Olaf Stapledon's 1937 novel *Star Maker*, in which the God-image is brought closer to our own consciousness as an evolving deity, who senses that we are more real than himself and so goes through a gradual awakening which reflects that of his creatures.

The voyages of the starship Enterprise and the Space Odyssey of Jupiter Two are journeys that are inner discoveries as well as outward adventures. As science fiction uses space travel as a vehicle for myth, in its quest 'to boldly go where no-one has gone before', it is still the individual who is a lens through which is focussed evolutionary challenges to the collective mind. Science fiction often concerns extraordinary individuals whose isolation and sense of destiny force them to transcend, or reject societal norms and embark on a quest for an authentic and meaningful identity. Through quest patterns intertwined with religious motifs such as the martyr, rebirth, the saviour, the repressed 'underpeople', and through mythic metaphors of ascent, descent, and the journey to the centre, science fiction explores the role of the individual as archetypal scapegoat, prophet, sacrifice, or mediator of the repressed, or rejected wisdom that is needed to advance human consciousness.

Some characters that come to mind here are the Martian Valentine in Heinlein's *Stranger in a Strange Land*, Rememberer Tomis in Robert Silverberg's *Nightwings*, Ransom in C. S. Lewis's space trilogy, Shevek in Le Guin's *The Dispossessed*, the 6-fold Gestalt unity in Sturgeon's *More Than Human*, Paul Atreides in *Dune*, John Keats in Dan Simmons' *Hyperion*, David Bowman in Clarke's *2010*, Courtney Hall in Ian McDonald's *Out on Blue Six*, Ender Wiggin in Orson Scott Card's *Speaker for the Dead*, the destitute, outcast woman Reah in Greg Bear's *Strength of Stones*, and in Clifford D. Simak's *Way Station* the humble, deaf-mute girl who, wielding a cosmic Talisman, becomes the new *mediatrix* of a universal spiritual force of peace and unity. To these we can add the Lion-man Painter in John Crowley's *Beasts*, the Tiger-woman Tigerishka in Fritz Leiber's *The Wanderer*, and the Catwoman C'mell in Cordwainer Smith's tales of the *Instrumentality of Mankind*. In these last few examples, culturally repressed irrationality and instinct are reintegrated into a vision of a wholesome self and society.

If life requires harmony, it also thrives on the creative tension of opposites from which unity arises. There is order, law and harmony in the cosmos, but there is also violence, emptiness and chaos. These, too, we must enter and transform into what is bearable. We must survive and transcend our own paradoxes before we can witness a rebirth of consciousness which will synthesise all fields of knowledge and experience. Science fiction deals with conflict in its many guises. But as Jung reminds us, a state of conflict is a sign of proximity to God, which translates into our need to embrace the dazzling darkness of ourselves.

In questioning the universe we will always face the vastness of mystery rather than a final revelation. In spite of this uncertainty, we cannot escape the gravity that pulls us toward a central singularity, an indescribable point within the boundless sphere of our existence. What we can be sure of is that this ball has well and truly stopped in our court, and we can never again pass it back to a rescuing deity. We are forgers of our own destiny; our horizons are boundless as we create and watch unfold the mythologisation of the cosmos.

AfterWords

The First Dream: Ayrton Senna [May 1994]

Dreams and visions play a vital role in my life and are as crucial to me as they were to Jung. There's a loose correlation between my initial Dream of Damien and the emotionally intense, ultra-real Dream I had of Formula One World Champion Ayrton Senna's fatal car crash, which I touch upon several times in the letters.

After speaking briefly with Damien, that night I had the Dream about us and a couple of months later began a relationship with him. In the case of Ayrton, I met him briefly at the 1993 Australian Grand Prix and roughly five months later — two months before I had my Dream of Damien — experienced his horrific crash.

Exactly thirty years later, I submitted an article about the Dream and events surrounding Ayrton's death to a prominent motor racing magazine. While the editors conceded that they'd enjoyed reading it, unsurprisingly they considered it to be too 'spiritual' for their target audience. Ironically, I had toned it down for their benefit, by omitting an account of how several years after Ayrton's death he 'turned up' in my astral energy field as a spiritual guide. There he has been a welcome presence ever since.

He has always sounded pretty much as he did in life, including his calm voice and the endearing way he quietly laughed. When I asked him, about twenty years ago, why he hadn't 'moved on', he replied that he'd chosen to return, to do as much good as he could. He's by no means always 'around'; my hunch is that he's been helping a lot of other people besides me. He also lives on in the hearts of millions, whose deep love for him is undying, and who still anguish over having lost him.

Now, lest I be accused of hailing from the lunatic fringe, let me make three things clear. Firstly, I have no pretensions to being a 'psychic', or (non-Jungian) 'medium' who channels spirits. I am, rather, more of a mediatrix to events unfolding in the collective unconscious, a gift that most likely arose from a 1983–4 acute spiritual crisis which sensitised me to the shared depths of the psyche. As a result, I'm often able to both detachedly observe and empathise with archetypal trends, collective emotions, and developments unfolding in the World Soul.

Secondly, I'm not implying that I hold any particular belief(s) about spiritual guides, or the afterlife. I'm simply confessing to an experienced mode of communion that for nearly three decades has been as real, effortless and natural to me as breathing. Thirdly — and as I know from decades of experience as a soul-centred psychiatric therapist — for many sufferers of schizophrenia, 'hearing voices' saps their energy and focus in a debilitating way, preventing them from engaging with the practical and relational demands of daily life. As well, such voices can become accusing, tormenting, tyrannical, or otherwise disruptive and unwelcome. Ayrton, on the other hand, has only ever been kind, encouraging, good-humoured, wise, unobtrusive, and supportive. He's helped me to stay focused, calm, disciplined, persevering, and appreciative of the sacredness of life and Nature. As an added blessing, he regularly makes me laugh about myself when I need to lighten up.

One can argue that such phenomena are manifestations of autonomous energies of the psyche only through circular reasoning that denies other possibilities, a step which Jung himself was never prepared to take. As he reminds us, we do not know the limits of the psyche. Make of it all what you will. For me, this gift is simply a treasured, mysterious and unquestioned part of my life. And in the end, my only certainty is that love knows no bounds.

On the eve of the new Millennium I asked Ayrton, should he be happy and free to do so, if he would meet me on the Other Side when I die. Straight away he answered, with a hint of mischief, 'Yes. I'll drive up in a white car and say, "Do you wanna come with me?"' As I recall, I burst into tears of amazed, anguished and joyful laughter. Roughly a decade later I came across a YouTube video in which Ayrton, in white socks and comfy moccasins, was preparing to test-drive a white Honda NSX car in Japan. As he was about to take off (at breakneck speed), he asked someone off-camera, 'Do you wanna come with me?'

And so without further ado, here is the article I produced for the 30th anniversary of Ayrton's death.

Encountering the Divinely Human: How Ayrton Senna Impacted My Life

I feel that there is a great force that brings me closer to God.... I have a chance to find harmony and to understand others.
Ayrton Senna [1989]

Early November, 1993. The Australian Formula One Grand Prix was once again being hosted in Adelaide. I was living in the inner eastern suburb of Beulah Park, within walking distance from the racetrack, a convenience offset by being forced to endure (when at home) the deafening roar of those raging F1 engines. A fellow postgraduate student, who'd been hired to work at the Grand Prix venue, had been granted a double pass to a pre-qualifying test morning that was closed to the wider public — and I was lucky to be invited along.

Arriving at the track, we found out that it was closed for checks and minor adjustments. Three time World Champion and winner of the 1991 Australian Grand Prix, Ayrton Senna, we were told, had not long ago completed some sort of test manoeuvre and was now busy consulting with McLaren mechanics in their garage. Since little else of significance seemed to be happening, as avid Senna fans we decided to head over to where we'd been told he was, in the vague hope of at least catching a glimpse of him.

Approaching the garage, we saw a group of people hovering outside. Our timing was impeccable. Ayrton, carrying a drink cup and evidently on a short break, suddenly emerged to autograph some photos, Grand Prix programs and crash helmets. Had the venue been open to the wider public we wouldn't have had a hope in hell of getting close to him; he would have been swamped by the media and fans. We hastened to join the group and I eventually found myself standing before him with a spare photo I had commandeered. Strange as it may sound, I felt like I was about to meet someone I already knew. Charming, friendly and gracious toward everyone around him, Ayrton was, as I later recounted in my diary, wearing a white t-shirt, the lower half of his red racing gear, the top jacket tied about his waist, and his iconic blue 'Ayrton Senna' cap.

As he handed back my signed photo, his hand touched mine. Without thinking I said, 'Thank you. May God be with you on Sunday. I'm hoping you'll win'. He smiled at me and with that wonderful Brazilian accent, said with good humour, 'That is very kind, thank you. For sure I'll be going for the win'. I was smitten. His face was beautiful, though not remotely effeminate, as if it were the outer expression of a soul who had perfectly married masculine strength, drive and courage to feminine tenderness and warmth.

I felt as if I'd shifted to another dimension. As someone who'd run spiritual retreats and worked for the Catholic Church as a pastor, I'd honed an instinct for reading other people's soul energy. I knew at once that I was in the presence of an exceptional human being. I was deeply moved. To this day, I've never encountered anyone with such a beautiful heart and luminous soul. I sensed that he was effortlessly at home with the divine, as if his twin passions of God and racing formed the very air he breathed, the water he loved to sail on, the soil he organically farmed on his communal family estate. My intuition was that he knew a deep empathy with Nature and humanity, not as something learned, or acquired, but as a rare gift deeply embedded in him at birth.

Ayrton radiated a subtly powerful aura that was calming, humble, sensitive, welcoming yet reclusive, confident yet shy, focused within yet at ease with everyone around him.

There was a stillness about him, which I suppose is a weird thing to say about someone capable of moving so fast. After a few minutes of signing photos, posters, programs and helmets, he cheerfully but firmly announced, 'OK. It's time for me to get back to work now'. Then he briefly waved and was gone.

Since my friend was scheduled to work that day at the venue, I decided to head back home, where I collected my car and drove to a printer's office to pick up newly bound copies of my finally completed PhD thesis. From there I headed to the city, where I officially submitted my 'labour of love' thesis to be examined in another state. And Ayrton, driving like a fierce angel with God, went on to win yet another Australian Grand Prix. Little did any of us know that it would be his last ever Formula One win.

The core theme of my thesis was what the great soul-centred psychiatrist C. G. Jung described as 'individuation', soul's ongoing circular journey toward a divinely centred wholeness of life. It's a winding path which unfolds only when we're completely true to the unique law of our own being, regardless of the personal cost. I've likened it to a twin-directional spiral: as consciousness spirals inward toward its still centre, its sphere of concerns at the same time spirals outward to embrace the world. That 'still centre' coincides with the heart, the core self where the love of truth meets the truth of love, while the circumferential whole of life is experienced as an empathic oneness with the World Soul.

Ayrton had, I felt, travelled a considerable distance in both directions along that double spiral. Perhaps that was one semi-conscious reason for his passionate love of racing; the twists and turns of the racing circuit are metaphors for life's unexpected changes of gear, pace, direction, scenery, and companions along the way. And crossing the finishing line means being back to square one, to the challenge of the next race. All in all, Ayrton was both true to his own journey as well as selflessly concerned for the welfare of others less fortunate than himself.

Nearly six months after meeting him, I had a Dream that was like having an archangelic spear driven through my heart. It was intensely vivid, overwhelming and traumatising. My consciousness was in a racing car as with frantic speed it navigated the twists and turns of the track. The car suddenly seemed to slow down and there was a sense of braking as it approached a curve. But instead of following the curve, the car kept going straight ahead and slammed into a high wall, hitting it at an angle with catastrophic, brutal force. There was a blindingly bright yet peaceful light and I was jolted awake by a deafening explosion and the sudden, colossal impact. I cried out, 'Ayrton, no, God, no, no, no'. I simply knew, beyond a shadow of doubt, that it was him. The sense of what I'd called out was, 'Dear God, no, please don't take this precious gift from the world'. But I already knew in my heart that God had called him home.

If you've ever had one of these very rare Dreams, you'll understand what I mean by saying that it tapped into a depth of absolute and ultimate certainty, a place of seamless unity, empathy and reality. This is the timeless, emotionally dense, shared realm of soul that C. G. Jung calls the 'collective unconscious'. When you fall into its ultra-real, overwhelming power and presence, it can resonate throughout your waking life like a destabilising time distortion and emotional tidal wave, as if a giant stone has fallen into your energy field and flung out enormous ripples that threaten to drag you into the Abyss, should you be unable to stay afloat above it.

Waking from the Dream was like returning to a lesser reality. My heart was pounding so hard that I feared it was about to burst. I felt like I was going to throw up. Disoriented and trembling, I got up and put on the TV, wondering if I'd see a news flash about Ayrton's crash. But nothing was announced. It was, as I recall, around 9.30 pm. I'd had a busy day and feeling tired, had gone to bed early. After turning off the TV I went back to bed, but couldn't sleep. I kept reliving the Dream, the blinding speed, the sudden braking, the horrific impact, the sense of annihilation, finality, loss, shock and explosive force – and the calmly brilliant light. I got up again around 10 pm and put on the TV. And there it was.

Ayrton had apparently just died on impact from massive head injuries during the San Marino Grand Prix, at the Imola circuit in Italy. Nonetheless he was being airlifted to hospital. Later released videos showed his blood dripping from the helicopter onto the roofs of cars below. The attending doctor reported some days later that Ayrton showed no brain activity after he'd been removed from the car, but because his heart was still beating he had been flown to hospital, where his heart gave out not long after.

I've never cried as gut-wrenchingly as I did while watching the TV coverage of Ayrton's death, since it wasn't news for me but rather an outer 'echo' of what I had in some deeper way experienced precognitively. I felt as if I'd lost a beloved friend, or relative immensely dear to me. Compounding the tragedy, when track officials examined the car wreckage they found a furled Austrian flag. Ayrton, who up until the crash had been leading the race, had planned to raise it after the race in honour of fellow driver Roland Ratzenberger, who had died in a fatal crash during a qualifying race on the previous day. (Upon learning of his death, Ayrton, inconsolable, had retreated to his motor home, broken down in tears and collapsed to the floor.)

A later technical report found that the steering column of Ayrton's car had fatigue cracks and had been badly welded together before the race. The consensus verdict is that during the seventh lap of the race it had snapped, causing him to lose control of the steering. The attending neurosurgeon, though not a religious man, claimed that he felt Ayrton's spirit depart as he lay on the ground after being removed from the car. His funeral procession a few days later, attended by three million people, was the largest ever in the city of Sao Paulo's history.

Two billion people were devastated to watch Ayrton's crash on live TV. Millions poured out emotional expressions of personal loss and anguish. The whole of Brazil imploded with grief and their government declared three days of national mourning.

Ayrton had always confessed that God was always with him, but that he felt closest to God while racing. Before each race he habitually reflected and sought guidance from a scripture reading. Before the San Marino race he allegedly prayed to God for the greatest gift that He could bestow. According to his sister, he was consoled by a Bible verse that assured him he would receive the greatest gift of all, God Himself.

For him, racing could be a path to transcendence, to an altered state of awareness that brought him beyond limited perception, something he once experienced (during a race) as driving well beyond normal human limits through a kind of tunnel. He realised he was no longer driving consciously, but rather by a kind of instinct in another spiritual dimension.

Ayrton always charted a razor thin track between the yin and yang of calmness and breathless speed, between discipline and danger, agony and triumph, humane sensitivity and indomitable will and inner fire. While in his presence at the

Australian Grand Prix, at first it had struck me as pleasantly surprising yet odd that this formidable competitor possessed such a calm demeanour, as well as such a kind gaze and gentle voice. Like the focused samurai, he drew strength and courage from inner poise and a humble sense of closeness to the divine. Years later it dawned in me that it was this lived paradox which made him — in words from the song Tina Turner dedicated to him at that Grand Prix — 'simply the best'. Beyond a doubt he was, and I suspect always will be, the most enigmatic, charismatic and beloved racing driver of all time.

He transcended the sport. As many people perceived, there was something ethereal, even mystical about him that was readily experienced by others, though impossible to define. You could see in his fathomless, supremely soulful gaze that inseparable blend of joy and sorrow that only fully alive individuals know. Yet at the same time Ayrton was always thoroughly grounded, practical, businesslike, and focused on his goals. Behind the wheel he was a ruthless, Zen-like warrior. Away from the track he enjoyed a contented life that included helping to run his family's organic farming estate. He was spiritual in this down-to-earth way, as if the divine both raced and rested in his blood.

Free of both pretence and false humility, he nonetheless had his flaws, as do we all. His often heated rivalry but later friendship with Alain Prost were legendary. He could be irritated, outspoken, anguished, annoying, or annoyed, when his striving for perfection and push for safer racing standards (on behalf of all racing drivers) at times drove him into conflict with race officials. Because of his dedication and meticulous attention to detail, he could be stubborn, insistent and relentless. He was a sincere, simple, yet wonderfully complex man.

Ayrton was also a hero. During the 1992 Belgian Grand Prix he stopped his car and risked his own life by running onto the circuit to save the life of fellow driver Erik Comas, who had crashed and ended up unconscious in the middle of the track.

His car was in danger of exploding and Ayrton turned off the ignition, then carefully held up Erik's head until the ambulance arrived. He was also a generous humanitarian. After his death it was discovered that he had donated hundreds of millions of dollars toward helping orphans and disadvantaged children, something he had kept secret throughout his life. Founded in the year he died, the Ayrton Senna Institute has since helped over 36 million Brazilian children.

It was some three years after he died — and after navigating the perils of an acute shamanic initiation crisis — that I experienced a series of similarly intense Dreams, again related to a horrendous car crash, this time the one which caused the death of Princess Diana. And as happened with Ayrton's death, millions of people all over the world poured out their grief, again feeling as if they'd lost a close friend, or dearly loved relative. For me, though, helping Diana was primarily pragmatic. I didn't experience her crash, but I had urgent, immediate shamanic work to do, to help her come to terms with the shock of finding herself suddenly dead and in a totally unfamiliar setting.

But Ayrton's death tore open my soul with profound emotion that, resonating through time, can still break me down into a rain of tears. And while I sense that Diana has well and truly 'moved on', my gut feeling is that Ayrton is somehow still around, as if through compassion he has taken on other work, perhaps aimed at helping to heal our wounded world.

From the age of four he followed his passion for racing, even though he later knew it could cost him his life. He did not believe — as Prost falsely claimed he did — that his faith in God made him immune to serious harm, or death. On the contrary, I feel deep down that he sensed the approach of death just before his fatal crash. You have only to watch the final video footage of him just before the race to see that he was, with a kind of resigned but peaceful sadness, already leaving us as he waited in his racing car. He looked calm, reflective, angelic, almost vulnerable, and only half there. It was haunting, but strangely beautiful. Sid Watkins, the delegated race doctor and Ayrton's close friend, had invited him to walk away from racing and come fishing instead, since as a World Champion he had nothing left to prove, but Ayrton replied, 'Sid, there are certain things over which we have no control. I cannot quit, I have to go on'.

This, to me, revealed an *archetypal* underpinning to his fate. It reminded me of the 'driven' girl in the Hans Christian Andersen fairytale, *The Red Shoes.* Once she'd put on the shoes, they danced her frantically though fields, rain, thorns and time with a kind of madness. She couldn't remove them — it was as if they'd become fused to her feet. Racing was like that for Ayrton. It was so deeply in his blood that it wouldn't release him but instead danced him into eternity. Yet in the here and now he is held securely in the hearts of those whose lives he touched.

Now and then the world receives the rare gift of an exquisite soul who can move the hearts of millions in a way that brings us closer to them, to the divine, and to each other. Ayrton Senna was one such divinely human gift. His death deeply wounded those who loved him, because that love made us vulnerable to the enduring pain of losing him. After his death, like countless others I never again watched Formula One racing. It was as if it had somehow lost its heart and soul.

When I feel a need for absolute tranquillity and safety, I sometimes journey shamanically to Ayrton's memorial garden statue and 'shrine' at Imola, where white doves sometimes flutter and visitors describe a surreal sense of serenity embedded in Nature. Here many colourful flags, posters, banners, floral tributes, Brazilian scarves and crash helmets are ritually placed and replaced in a steady stream of quiet devotion that shows no sign of abating, thirty years after Ayrton's death. It's a truly magical and uniquely peaceful 'sacred space'.

And now for the kicker: a few hours before Ayrton died, my PhD supervisor rang to let me know that my thesis had been accepted by both examiners. And so on the day I submitted my thesis, I met Ayrton Senna. And on the bittersweet day he died, May 1 1994, I was awarded my PhD degree. Since then I have lit a candle on every anniversary of his death. Though as is widely rumoured among F1 devotees, 'Ayrton never died. He's just a lap ahead of the rest of us'.

1 May, 2024

Final Dreams: Princess Diana [August 1997]

Both Ayrton and Princess Diana were 'of the people' and for the people. Diana, like Ayrton, was always warm, friendly and accessible to an adoring public who were drawn to her like moths to a flame. Like Ayrton, she also did whatever she could to help and support those less fortunate than herself. Following her tragic death in Paris, the worldwide outpouring of grief was similar to that which attended the loss of Ayrton. Millions of men, women and children wept in the streets, for themselves as well as for the beloved icons they had lost. Cards, photos, candles and personal letters were ritually placed at key places of remembrance. My intuition is that it was the intensity of this shared grief which triggered my access to the emotional depths of the global World Soul, which in turn erupted into my powerful Dreams of Diana and Ayrton.

My first Dream of Diana took place after I had gone through a shamanic initiation crisis and subsequent training. I was having a quiet, afternoon sleep after a morning of intensive therapy work. Once in the Dream, I found myself in a kind of neutral ground, or in-between place; it was quiet and supremely functional. Scattered throughout what felt like a sacred space were baths, small temples, meandering pathways, streams, comfortable robes and towels. It was something like an ancient

Greek garden, but with no sense of 'heaven'; rather, it was a low-key, peaceful place for getting done what needed to be done there and then. It wasn't like any other place I've visited in dreams, or shamanic journeying, but featured lots of off-white stoneware, and robed folk wandering about in twos and threes, absorbed in their own business. The Dream was ritualistically atmospheric rather than merely visual, and the sense of personal communion was overwhelming and deeply moving.

Throughout this long Dream, I felt very close to Diana after she joined me and we slowly made our way to one of the small temples. Once inside, as part of a healing ritual I helped to wash blood off of her into a large, square, white bath. I remember watching the blood swirl clockwise around and down the plug-hole, while at the same time we were talking in detail about the irreversibility of what had happened to her, and about the reality of the here and now. We'd also talked about all this while making our way across the grounds. She found it hard to accept that she could not yet leave the place where we were, or that she was in fact dead. She was not overly distressed; more like puzzled, tired, and regretful, but the main focus of the dream was on the healing of her soul and body, and on my offer to take upon myself her woundedness.

There was no particular point at which this happened, but suddenly I began to feel physically badly hurt, weak, and aching, as if I were recovering from a recent and devastating major operation. I looked down the front of my body, which was badly bruised from the upper chest area, and a huge, healing scar was running down my body. The scar was like a long clean scalpel cut, a thin line that was already closed up. I felt a kind of wonderment at this, partly, I recall, because in a relieved way I'd taken on the woundedness in a kind of recovery mode, without having endured the initial shock and horror of the wound's infliction. I remember that this ritualistic work — helping Diana wash herself free of blood, talking through what was now real, and feeling wounded — was re-enacted several times, until there was an acceptance by her of death, after which I was free to leave her in peace and in the care of others. What I next recall is that I was awoken by the phone ringing. A close friend had called to ask if I'd heard the news of Diana's terrible crash.

I can't describe the kind of closeness that this Dream involved. It wasn't what you'd call friendship, or sisterliness, or motherliness; it was (for want of better words) an indefinable sense of solidarity, sorrow, patience, and compassion. For the next couple of days I felt an aching grief and could not focus on any work, but I also felt at peace and glad that I'd been able to help Diana.

Shamans are often called upon to lead or escort the dead, or to help them cross over to the afterlife. In the Dream I was, in this sense, being called upon to help a suffering, shocked and bewildered soul come to terms with death. As anthropologist Mircea Eliade notes, the shaman is vital when the dead person is reluctant to forsake the realm of the living, or when the deceased finds it too hard to journey alone to the beyond. Here only the shaman possesses the power of the *psychopomp*, or soul-guide, who like the Greek Hermes and the Egyptian Anubis escorts and converses with the dead. In the case of Diana, her mode of death was so traumatic and sudden, and involved such deep bodily wounding that she was understandably disoriented, weakened and confused when she found herself to be suddenly dead and in a strange place.

I'm reminded here of Jung's comments late in life about death, when he suggested that it was a *mysterium coniunctionis*, a marriage, or union through which the soul finally regains its lost wholeness. Archetypal and shamanic, in other words, are not mutually exclusive, since both involve a communion with transcendent reality. It may well be that what shamans talk about as visits to Overworld and Underworld realms of gods and spirits — and what others describe as accessing the archetypal realm through visions and altered states of consciousness — are different ways of describing the same kinds of experience. As well, archetypal experiences, which usually have a powerful emotional resonance, are well able to deeply impact both the individual and collective psyche.

Reflecting several days later on the Dream, I was moved by two key images: the blood spiralling clockwise into the white bath, and my own woundedness. The first image resonates with the symbolism of the 'alchemical bath', a ritual baptism, symbolic death, or purification ritual for the sacred marriage as the divine wedding of masculine and feminine energies within the individual and the world. The bath precedes a spiritual rebirth, or transformation through which the solar and lunar opposites, imaged as red (male) and white (female), are united through a cyclic flow of these complementary energies.

Jung understood alchemy to be a symbolic paradigm of the journey toward wholeness which he called 'individuation'. Through an oscillation between separation and synthesis, or disintegration and integration, the psyche undergoes a cyclic transformation that marries the opposing energies of life and in doing finds ultimate value and harmony. As Jung made clear, individuation eventually 'gathers the world to itself', hence the final alchemical 'Holy Grail' involves becoming one with an underlying unitary reality, through a merging of one's personal path (or Tao) with universal Tao. The complementary energies of life can be alchemically symbolised in many ways: as gold and silver, sun and moon, king and queen, red and white, spirit and matter, fire and water, earth and air.

The Dream imagery also resonates with a medieval alchemical picture of Christ — a symbol of the 'divine self' as Wounded Healer and King — sitting in the round baptismal bath of life, flanked on either side by the alchemical King and Queen, and the Sun and Moon, and pierced through the side with a spear. From the wound, blood pours into the bath, while from the upper right corner, from a wine press, wine as the 'Water of Life', or *aqua vitae* flows into the bath.

In the Dream, in other words, Diana is a symbolic counterpart to Christ, such that a 'Queen of People's Hearts' has now also become a symbol of the divine self. Through this ritualistic gesture, the feminine side of the God-image is reinstated and reunited with its masculine half, anticipating a condition of restored *wholeness*, both within the individual and in the World Soul. Because of this archetypal content, the Dream also meets the criteria for what some native cultures recognise and C. G. Jung describes as a 'Big Dream', as a vitally important, symbolic message for the world.

Jung understood that a deep wound to the Western psyche had been inflicted through the feminine being driven insane by patriarchal *hubris* and intellectualism. Diana was very much the antithesis of this patriarchal bias; in spite of her flaws and insecurities she was humble and guided not by intellect, theoretical beliefs and aggressive ambition, but by her humanitarian values and empathic heart. Often accused of being 'disturbed', or 'borderline', she was driven to desperation and anguish by the conflict between demanding public duty to the rigid, patriarchal institution which her husband embodied — and a deeper need to follow her heart.

As a kind of human Goddess, she helped to heal the Western moralistic split in the Goddess image, through which the Goddess is portrayed as either virginal, or whorish and 'fallen'. Perhaps the best example here is the Christian schism between the Virgin Mary and Mary Magdalene, even though there is no evidence that the latter was a prostitute. In recent times, this projection onto her was undermined through Dan Brown's novel *The Da Vinci Code*, in which Mary Magdalene is revealed to be the wife of Christ and the mother of his child.

Diana similarly became the recipient of moralistic cultural projections. She was imaged at first as a chaste and pure maiden, but later seen as a flawed and sexual woman, unreachable (as a Goddess) yet touchable and fully human. Like the Gnostic Sophia she fell from her royal position into the world, where she was forced to wander alone and struggle to be reunited with her lost masculine half. She achieved this not by re-marrying, but by attuning to her own inner masculine strength, and in so doing became more confident, outspoken, discerning, courageous, independent, in a word, whole. Yet she retained her vulnerability and compassion, becoming a queen of people's hearts. Her death as a kind of sacrifice meant that we were no longer free to project onto her the shift in consciousness which she embodied. We were then each left to choose between owning in ourselves what she incarnated — the humanising of the divine feminine — or mourning a lost ideal, leaving it fated to sink back into the Goddess's Lake like the Arthurian sword Excalibur, from where it would later arise again. For the Goddess as life-in-death Phoenix will always find a way to turn tears into a panacea for the world's ills, through embracing suffering as a catalyst for the rebirthing of herself.

My final Dreams of Diana were thankfully joyful. In my second, short Dream of her, I was checking in to see how she was faring. I was pleased to discover her happily engrossed in practising ballet steps and so left her in contented peace. In my final Dream of her, we were standing at the shore of a beautiful, still lake that lay in the midst of a tranquil valley. I asked her if she felt like taking a walk across the water. She did, and as I led the way she tentatively followed.

Fierce Angel

If my heart could swim in fire
if I could go back to that fateful time
and beg you not to be for just one day
the driven fierce angel you are
If I could tell you what you already suspected to be true

that the daring dance was not unfolding
petals one by one instead were torn
until the blood red rose was ruined
But nothing could unbind you from
the love that drove your racing heart
no-one could persuade you just to walk away
And so that night I dreamed you could not hold the curve
but took instead a path beyond my reach
at least in that last lap which brought
the billions breaking to their knees
Simply the best unfading bloom
is now caressed beneath your final falling gaze
And so I go there when I can
where white doves brush the shadows
from the light that holds you still
and my soul reclines in yours
as if at home for the last time

[MBR/for Ayrton, 1/5/2024]

Author Biography

As a 'New Renaissance' individual, Maureen B. Roberts has worked, studied, created and taught in a broad variety of interweaving fields. Over several decades she has widely published non-fiction papers and artwork in the arenas of Jungian psychology, contemporary mythology, and shamanism. For the past thirty years she has run a private practice as a depth and shamanic psychotherapist, but has now retired to focus on both fiction and non-fiction writing projects.

Maureen has won two university literary prizes: The Sir Archibald Strong Memorial Prize for Literature, and The Edith Hubbe and Harriet Cook Prize. She holds a PhD in the hybrid field of English Literature and Jungian Psychology, and also studied astronomy as part of a university science degree.

Dr Roberts has worked as an editor, PhD thesis examiner, recording and performance singer, songwriter and musician, gardener, pastoral care worker, ecological surveyor, spiritual retreat guide, graphic artist and photographer. In 1986 she assisted pre-eminent Australian photographer William Yang in his coverage of the Adelaide Festival of Arts.

As a university and adult education tutor, Maureen has taught courses on science fiction, creative stencilling, astronomy, literature, crystal healing, technical communication, Jungian psychology, and Medicine Wheel work. In addition to hosting her own radio show and being a regular guest on ABC Radio, Maureen has been a speaker at conferences and seminars run by The Mythopoeic Literature Society of Australia, The Theosophical Society, Voices Victoria [schizophrenia support network], the C. G. Jung Society of South Australia, and the Mental Health ReEducation and Human Rights Network.

Dr Roberts ran Australia's Schizophrenia Drug-free Crisis Centre from 2002–11. In place of solicitors, she has represented victims of coercive psychiatry at Brisbane Supreme Court trials, and at South Australian Guardianship Board hearings. She has also been flown overseas and interstate by relatives of loved ones in acute psychospiritual crises, who were desperate for soul-centred alternatives to biopsychiatry. In 2002 she convened 'Soul Down Under', Australia's first international conference on residential and drug-free crisis care for psychosis.

Maureen lives in a small cottage in a quiet country village near the sea, on South Australia's beautiful Fleurieu Peninsula, where she enjoys campervan trips, gardening, fire circles and music jams with friends, creating organic healthcare products, and coastal bushwalking.

6TH
BOOKS

ALL THINGS PARANORMAL

Investigations, explanations and deliberations on the paranormal, supernatural, explainable or unexplainable. 6th Books seeks to give answers while nourishing the soul: whether making use of the scientific model or anecdotal and fun, but always beautifully written.

Titles cover everything within parapsychology: how to, lifestyles, alternative medicine, beliefs, myths and theories.

If you have enjoyed this book, why not tell other readers by posting a review on your preferred book site?

Phantoms of Christmas Past
Paul Weatherhead
True stories of seasonal ghost hoaxes and strange phantom panics from the nineteenth and early twentieth centuries.
Paperback: 978-1-80341-840-7 ebook: 978-1-80341-866-7

Spirit Release
Sue Allen
A guide to psychic attack, curses, witchcraft, spirit attachment, possession, soul retrieval, haunting, deliverance, exorcism and more, as taught at the College of Psychic Studies.
Paperback: 978-1-84694-033-0 ebook: 978-1-84694-651-6

Advanced Psychic Development
Becky Walsh
Learn how to practise as a professional, contemporary spiritual medium.
Paperback: 978-1-84694-062-0 ebook: 978-1-78099-941-8

Where After
Mariel Forde Clarke
A journey that will compel readers to view life after death in a completely different way.
Paperback: 978-1-78904-617-5 ebook: 978-1-78904-618-2

Paranormal Perspectives: One Big Box of 'Paranormal Tricks'?

John Fraser

Think Zen and the Art of Spending the Night in a Haunted House, a celebration of the dream of finding something undiscovered and different.

Paperback: 978-1-80341-524-6 ebook: 978-1-80341-532-1

Haunted: Horror of Haverfordwest

G.L. Davies

Blissful beginnings for a young couple turn into a nightmare after purchasing their dream home in Wales in 1989.

Paperback: 978-1-78535-843-2 ebook: 978-1-78535-844-9

Astral Projection Made Easy and overcoming the fear of death

Stephanie June Sorrell

From the popular Made Easy series, Astral Projection Made Easy helps to eliminate the fear of death through discussion of life beyond the physical body.

Paperback: 978-1-84694-611-0 ebook: 978-1-78099-225-9

Developing Your Supernatural Awareness

Fredrick Woodard

The common themes and details pointed out in this book will develop or enhance your understanding of our supernatural awareness and connection with our interactive universe.

Paperback: 978-1-80341-478-2 ebook: 978-1-80341-479-9

Readers of ebooks can buy or view any of these bestsellers by clicking on the live link in the title. Most titles are published in paperback and as an ebook. Paperbacks are available in traditional bookshops. Both print and ebook formats are available online.

Find more titles and sign up to our readers' newsletter at **www.6th-books.com**

Join the 6th books Facebook group at **6th Books The world of the Paranormal**